TRANSGENDERING FAITH

TRANSGENDERING
FAITH

Identity, Sexuality, and Spirituality

Leanne McCall Tigert and Maren C. Tirabassi, editors

THE PILGRIM PRESS

CLEVELAND

The Pilgrim Press, 700 Prospect Avenue, Cleveland, Ohio 44115-1100
thepilgrimpress.com

Printed in the United States of America on acid-free paper

09   08   07   06   05   04   5   4   3   2   1

Library of Congress Cataloging-in-Publication Data

Transgendering faith : identity, sexuality, and spirituality / Leanne McCall Tigert
    and Maren C. Tirabassi, editors.
        p.   cm.
    Includes bibliographical references.
    ISBN 0-8298-1494-9 (paperback. : alk. paper)
    1. Transsexualism—Religious aspects—Christianity.   2. Christian transsex-
uals—Religious life.   I. Tigert, Leanne McCall, 1957–   II. Tirabassi, Maren C.

BR115.T76T73   2004
261.8'35768—dc22
                                                        2004053519

CONTENTS

FOREWORD
GIVING THANKS FOR WHO WE ARE

"Dear God, please help me stop doing this terrible thing." I remember as a young child—and, yes, as an adult, too—the many times I got on my knees to ask God to remove from my soul the "curse" of being transgendered.

Today, I am able to thank my God for the gift I have been given as a transgender person. And I am thrilled that I can write this prelude to a book that celebrates the transgender experience in words, rites, poetry, and ritual.

When I was a child, I didn't know I was transgender. We didn't have the vocabulary that has grown up over the past decades and I didn't have anybody to turn to who could tell me what this adversity was and why I had been afflicted by it. I couldn't talk to my mother; as a widow she had her hands full with raising four children and didn't need the additional burden of my dark secret. I couldn't talk to our family doctor; he didn't have the background to deal with these kinds of issues. And, most sadly, I couldn't talk to my priest; he could only tell me my thoughts were impure and my actions sinful—stop them!

So I struggled through childhood, teen age and adult life with the implicit understanding that I was "sinful" and "bad." What a horrible thing for any person to have to deal with.

It was particularly difficult because, as a young person, I wanted so to be a "good" person. I loved God and wanted to be a priest. But, obviously, the world was telling me I had a defect that wouldn't allow me to follow that dream.

For nearly sixty years, I struggled with God over this "curse." I was alone with a secret that would devastate my family and friends and nothing seemed to work in making it go away. Then, one of my sons, by now grown and engaged in his career as a psychotherapist, asked me what was going on in my life—why I seemed so different than I used to be, so angry and detached.

I took a deep breath and told him. "I am transgendered."

After lots of tears and talk, he asked me to see a therapist. There for the first time I was able to tell someone all of the things that had been going on in my head for all of these years. She helped me to understand that being transgendered wasn't a defect; it was just another variation among the myriad ways that God has created us. This wasn't a curse.

In fact, I have come to understand that God has touched me. What I thought was an affliction was really a blessing. The insights that have come to me from this struggle over my gender issues have led me to new places in my spiritual life and to new levels of involvement in the lesbian-gay-bisexual-transgendered (LGBT) community.

These nights my prayers are distinctly different from what they have been.

"Dear God, thank you for the gifts you have given me and help me to make the most of them in my life and in the lives of others."

I hope that the stories, poems, rites, and rituals contained in this book will help transgender people better understand themselves and bring them to an understanding of how blessed they—we—are in the eyes of God, our Creator.

—Barbara Satin,
Moderator of United Church of Christ
Coalition for LGBT Concerns

ACKNOWLEDGEMENTS

IN THE CONTEXT OF THIS BOOK, Leanne and Maren have served as theologians, liturgists, and editors. While Leanne has spent hours in psychotherapy with clients working to free themselves from cultural and religious constraints, Maren has served as a local church pastor trying to help congregations become safer places for gender minorities and allies. In both of these contexts, unchallenged questions, fears, and confusion can build into defensive bigotry. However, these same questions, fears, and confusions can also become the birthplaces of empathy and compassion. The response of a local congregation and its clergy and lay leadership can make all the difference.

As editors, we came together two years ago, wanting to offer the voices of transgender people of faith, and to create a "user-friendly" compilation of worship resources, Bible study, and information for further study. This book is for individuals who may see themselves reflected in some of these stories. It is also for congregations in the hope that our churches do not miss out on the incredible gifts of faithful people, which are there to be received.

In the process of shaping this book, we have certainly received some remarkable gifts of grace. We are extremely indebted to each of the writers in this book. They have shared their life journeys with us in the hope that their stories will benefit others. Each of these contributions is extremely personal and vulnerable. We are honored to be a part of this process, and trust that you will find these stories to be as sacred texts, filled with truth and inspiration.

We are also indebted to others who have helped us in this journey: Rev. Carole Carlson for her counsel, Peter Johnston, who created our flier, Karan Parkin for creating our web page, the United Church Coalition for LGBT Concerns, UCC conference ministers and MCC clergy who helped spread the word about this book, Kim Sadler, our editor, and our dear families, patient with meeting times and free with advice—Don, Matt, Maria, Julia and Emily, Rachel, and Sarah.

We offer this book in the hope that people will no longer be held captive in the terror of silence in the pews and pulpits of our congregations.

Part One

THE BASICS FOR EVERYONE

TRANS-LATING
WHAT, AND FOR WHOM?

L E A N N E   M C C A L L   T I G E R T

WHEN I WAS FIFTEEN YEARS OLD, my mother and I stopped at a Burger King one day for lunch. She stayed in the car while I went in to order take-out. I was wearing overalls, a flowered cotton shirt, and sneakers (the uniform of the seventies). Returning to the car with food in hand, I opened the door and sat down in the passenger's seat. My mother turned toward me with a look of horror.

"Leanne, you should be ashamed of yourself."

"Huh?" I had no clue what she was talking about.

"People in the restaurant were staring at you. They couldn't tell if you were a boy or a girl. Shame on you."

My heart dropped through the floorboard. She was right. People did stare at me. My stomach churned. I wanted to throw up. I felt bad, wrong, crazy. Then the rage hit, and my head began to silently explode.

"What the hell is wrong with them? With me? With you, Mom. Why are you so embarrassed by me? Why do people watch me, sometimes with disgust on their face, and sometimes with amusement? What gives them the right to stare at me, open mouthed. Why doesn't someone say, 'You should be ashamed of yourselves' to them? And why does it make me feel so horrible, so wrong, so disgusting? I can't help the way I was born. I can't help that my facial features are so masculine that people think I'm a boy, unless I dress up. And why does it make me want to run away, disappear, from everyone? Why did God make me like this?"

This particular scenario has repeated itself numerous times throughout my life. My body type and facial structure, the way I carry myself, the clothes I am most comfortable in have always been androgynous. I have observed over the years that many of my lesbian and heterosexual women friends can wear men's polo shirts and khaki pants without others staring or questioning their gender. When I wear something similar, people stare. Just the other day I was at the shopping mall with my two daughters, buying clothes for summer camp. I was wearing a long sleeved tee shirt, shorts, and sandals. As I walked through the mall, I caught the eye of a middle-age man watching me. The look I saw was familiar—amusement, curiosity, nervousness. As I continued to walk, I became more watchful. Yes, people were staring at me, just like they did when I was six, and fifteen, and thirty-five. Yes, I no longer feel shame, but sometimes I still feel rage, and the questions: "Do my kids notice this? Are they embarrassed? What is it about our society that allows people to stare, either with contempt or curiosity, at individuals who step outside of the prescribed gender norms of our culture? Why is this so volatile? Why is it so scary? What is the source of shame that cuts deep?"

As Virginia Ramey Mollenkott says, "Our society is currently ruled by a binary gender construct: a largely unquestioned set of assumptions that there are only two sexes (male and female). . . . Either a person must self-define as exclusively male or female, or else admit to being unnatural, mutant, or abnormal."[1]

I have been working as an activist for LGBT rights in both the church and society since the 1980s. During the first decade of that work I was oblivious to the needs of transgender persons, or the importance of trans-liberation to the whole Christian community. However, throughout the past ten years, more transgender people have been courageously stepping out of the closet and demanding the justice and liberation that is rightly theirs. Yet at the same time, I hear various gay, lesbian, bisexual, and heterosexual persons make statements like, "Well, I understand people being gay, but this is too much," or "They don't belong in our equal rights movement. We've worked too hard, and they'll just slow us down," or "Don't push us. We've taken on enough in this church." Our memories are often short. These are the same kinds of statements made about any struggle for justice. For example, "While we're working towards equality for women, let's not mention lesbians—it will just raise more controversy," or "Mentioning bisexuality will just make people nervous," or "Let's not bring up racism in this gay event." Our memories are even shorter when it comes to the role of transgender persons in the work of sexual liberation. Each year, hundreds of thousands of LGBT persons and allies march in gay pride parades commemorating the Stonewall riots. The Stonewall Inn was a "drag" club in New York City that was often raided by police. On this particular night in June, 1969, many transgender persons fought back and were arrested, fueling the energy for the work of LGBT liberation to this day.

As an activist within the United Church of Christ, I have had the opportunity to speak with many local churches about the needs and gifts of LGBT persons within the church. Often, I have been invited to a diaconate meeting or adult study group as they engage in the Open and Affirming study process (a curriculum of the United Church Coalition for Lesbian, Gay, Bisexual, Transgender Concerns). I have worked with large urban congregations, suburban, small town, and rural parishes. Sometimes when I attend a discussion, I receive a phone call from a church member on the following day. Often, this person is transgender or has a spouse who is. The fear of coming out, combined with the relief of speaking honestly to a church person, is palpable through the phone line. I always ask if he/she has spoken with his/her pastor. Usually the response is, "Are you kidding? No way!" Even if I know the pastor and reassure the parishioner that the conversation would be affirming and confidential, there is hesitation. Even if the church is talking more openly about sexual orientation, regarding gender identity it remains silent. When the church is silent, oppression festers and grows.

Transgender persons experience more oppression than perhaps any nontransperson can imagine. I was speaking with a female-to-male trans gender man the other day. He has felt completely male in his mind since young childhood. He has never considered a physical transition through hormone therapy or surgery even though he says, "There is not one female bone in my body." He won't transition because he can't bear to lose contact with his family of origin. He is sure that they will completely cut him off. Considering that they won't talk about his female life partner, or his perceived lesbian identity (as they think of him as a woman), he is probably right. At work, everyone thinks he is a lesbian, because he has a very masculine appearance in a biologically female body, and a female partner. He is sure that he would loose his job if he came out as transgender. Without family, money, or work, how would he survive? Thus, he has chosen to live with this complete divide between his brain and body. He chooses to remain asexual stating that, "When someone touches my vagina or breasts, it feels like a rape, no matter how much she loves me. It's not right. It's not me. It just reminds me how wrong my body is, and it makes me feel sick. So, I give it up. I don't talk about it, and just try to be a good person."

I have spent many psychotherapy hours with clients trying to determine whether they would be able to handle the consequences of going out in public as their true selves. Questions such as, "How do I handle the ridicule? What bathroom do I use? Will I be physically safe? What if someone becomes violent towards me? What if the police stop me for speeding? What will they do to me? I can't get thrown into a jail cell with others—I won't survive!" These are the questions one must address just to go out for an evening, let alone begin the full transitioning process.

Transgender people are targets for ridicule and violence in our society. The above questions are just the beginning. Imagine being perceived as biologically male and dressed as a women to drive to a transgender support group. What happens if you have a car accident and end up in the emergency room of the local hospital? Can you trust that you would be given the same care by the medical staff as you would if you were not cross-dressed? What if you get picked up for DWI after leaving a bar, and get taken to a holding cell with other men? How would you cope? The rate of physical and sexual assault and violence against transgender persons is significantly higher than it is for lesbian, gay, or bisexual persons. Usually, the crimes are brutal. Crimes against male-to-female transpersons have been reported as particularly violent, including multiple stabbings and rape, and being hit and repeatedly run over by cars. Obviously, a society still bound by patriarchy feels particularly threatened when men choose womanhood over their masculine role. The perpetrators of these crimes often feel as though they are enforcing the norms of society and religion.

Lisa Hartley, one of the writers in this collection, said to me, "The biggest sex organ we have is the brain. Thus, the genitals are superficial." Think about it: if someone took away your penis or vagina, you would still be who you are. If you are not transgender, you would still identify as male or female, as you always had. Your chromosomes and hormones would be unchanged. You are the same person, with or without your sexual genitalia. If you are transgender, your brain is one sex and your body is another. Thus, you have to decide whether to modify your body, or adjust your behavior, because you cannot change your brain. There is good information about the science and biology of gender identity, as well as the sociology of gender construction available for those who would like to know more. Some resources are suggested in the appendix of this book.

Just as with any issue of diversity, we are not talking about people "out there" and removed from the life of the church. We are talking about deacons, Sunday school teachers, choir members. We are talking about the family members of transgender persons who sit silently in the pews, holding in their confusion and isolation, and we are talking about clergy, who sometimes have good will but, because of the silence on this issue in churches and seminaries, have little information. Transgender liberation is not just about freeing persons whose body and brain are mismatched. It is about finding the true soul within each of us, unbound and unconstricted by social constructs and religious norms. It is about moving beyond divisive categories, and moving into a more fluid and honest sexuality. It is about liberation—body, brain, soul, personal, and societal. It is about the work and word of God.

NOTES

1. Virgina Ramey Mollenkott, "Gender Diversity and Christian Community, *Transgender Pocket,* 2000, the UCC Coalition for Lesbian, Gay, Bisexual, and Transgender Concerns.

2

CULTURALLY INDUCED STRESS
IT ONLY HURTS BECAUSE YOU ARE DIFFERENT

LISA M. HARTLEY, ACSW-DCSW

THE TRANSGENDER COMMUNITY HAS COME A LONG WAY. Think of how it was ten years ago—in 1994. For those of you who do recall, what did you experience? What was it like? What is different today? Is it better or worse?

Today, we have experienced an increase in recognition, that is, positive recognition. There are more legal protections from discrimination. More than fifty cities (including Boston and New York) and two states have included protections for transgendered people. People are transitioning on the job. Faith communities are reaching out to transgendered people, especially the Unitarian Universalist and United Church of Christ communities. Ten years ago we didn't know how transgender happened. We certainly disagreed with those who said we were psychiatrically disturbed. Today, we have a host of studies that bring us ever closer to understanding just what transgender is and how it develops.

We know from research that our brain is the place of our true sex identity—not our genitals as has been believed in the past. The hypothalamus seems a central arena of research focus concerning sex identity and behavior. Still, there are questions to be answered. Is transgender inborn ("hard-wired")? What is the role of hormones in sex identity? Is the BSTc [a section of the hypothalmus] in the brain the site of everyone's sex identity? Is there a genetic reason for transgender? How come some of us are content to cross-dress, while others must live full time in the "opposite" gender role, and still others must completely transition to the "other" sex identity and assume the gender role associated with that sex identity? These, and other questions, still await explanation. We can say that a physical reason is certainly present—a physical reason that translates into transgender. Yet, can research reports really help people accept our being different? If so, how much impact does research have?

So, if things are going so well, why do I continue the tome: "Culturally Induced Stress" (CIS), It Only Hurts Because You Are Different"? Because things are better, we can now take a look at the process of becoming to improve our lives and the lives of those who have yet to come after us.

BEING DIFFERENT

We have been portrayed in the media in many ways; from Mrs. Doubtfire to Branden Teena, from a college professor on "The Education of Max Bicford," to the cross-dressed brother on the Drew Carey show. We have been coming out in greater numbers and have experienced success in becoming integrated in mainstream culture. All is not rosy, to be sure, but there is less fear of us, now that people have seen us more and more. Allies, supporters, and friends and families have joined our advocacy journey for recognition and a place in the world. Have you seen Christina Aguilera's video for her song "Beautiful?" The recent national survey done by the Human Rights Commission has also given us reason to feel optimistic.

Yet, even with the physical nature of transgender very possibly identified, there are still the challenges within our own minds, and within the minds of others around us.

So—how are things for *you*? Are they going great? Could things be better? And what about *you*?—do you feel comfortable with who you are? Is there anything that you worry about? Acceptance? Family? Regrets? Anger? Fears? Resignation to some losses? Loneliness? Let's face it—we are different. Sometimes that is beautiful. Sometimes it is a source of anxiety. Sometimes . . .

What does being different mean to you? Is it good? Bad? Healthy? Does it reflect our vulnerability?

CHALLENGES WE FACE

From the moment of our birth we are identified by others who define us by sex: the person who delivers us at birth, by looking at our genitals, our parent(s), who choose our name and dream of how we will "turn out." The record of our birth is the binding legal statement that says who we are.

We are socialized immediately, and later taught "proper" behavior. We learn to recognize our parent(s) and siblings, and learn how to eat, speak, walk, and control our bladder and bowels, all within the first three years of life! We learn what is important. We learn that we are part of a family. We learn loyalty to the family culture, including the family's race and ethnicity. We also learn about our family secrets and learn to keep them secret. We are praised for doing "good," and punished for being "bad." In general, "socialization" efforts by those around us are very intensive, especially between birth and age five. And when we are not being actively taught, we watch, and listen, and integrate everything we see and hear within our very core, so that we can know just how to "be." Like everyone else, we desperately want to please and receive praise.

Then there comes this feeling, this desire to be the other sex. This frightens us and challenges everything that we have learned. We worry about ourselves. We fear others might find out. Prayers do not help. We become angry with ourselves in having these thoughts and desires. Yet, we must press on, hoping it will go away. But it doesn't go away. It just gets "worse." We wonder, am I crazy? Am I gay or lesbian? Why do I enjoy "dressing up?"

Perhaps you have seen the movie *36 Hours,* a 1964 film in which James Garner plays the role of a WW II U.S. army officer who has been captured by the Germans. They brainwash him into believing that the war is over, hoping that he will believe it and tell them what he knows about troop movements.

Like James Garner, we are "brainwashed" into our reality. Of course, we don't call it brainwashing! We call it "socialization." We are told what sex we are, and how to check it out—that is, look at the genitals. Certain things are okay for us. Other things are sacred to the *other* sex and are strictly off limits.

In the movie, James Garner is almost fooled. But at one point, he somehow gets some salt on his hand. When it stings, he realizes that a paper cut happened to him just before being captured. Then he knows that the date that he was given by his captors had to be false. In the end he gives wrong information and manages to escape to freedom.

Our realization that we have been misidentified happens usually around age four or five, and for some of us, it happens at least by the time before puberty begins. We are ill equipped to know what to do, so we play along with the "authorities." Our journey is lonely and filled with anxiety. We punish ourselves for being different. We feel a lowered sense of self-esteem because we are not like the others. But we press on, and on, and on. We have "heard the music" but have not found the words—yet.

One day we find some words, and then some more. We realize that we are not alone, and that there are others who share the same transgender journey that we experience. Then we make a friend, like us! "Take it easy. Don't go so fast." We find a support group. There are then more words and examples of how to do it. Then a trial run cross-dressed; then another. Oh, God, we are different, that's for sure. People stare but they don't laugh. Wow, we made it safely to the other end of the mall!

But all the fears and all the worries that we are not doing what we were taught to do, continue to haunt us. We wonder when retribution will come. The music is there. The words are there. The feelings of victory over finally understanding that we were given the wrong sex identification, followed by socialization appropriate to the wrong sex identity. But still we fear. Still we await retribution, like a child that has spilled milk on the floor.

We feel different because we have challenged the most concentrated behavioral training that human beings can experience—"socialization." We have learned that different is bad. That is why we fear retribution. That is why we expect it.

And there *are* instances of retribution. Transgendered people are killed. Transgendered people are assaulted. Practically every transgendered person will experience social embarrassment(s). Transgendered people do lose their jobs. Many times a transgendered person's family rejects them. On and on, the examples come. And we wonder, what will be our price for being different?

But we cannot hide any longer. We must come out. We must "be" or cease to "be." Good thing there is back-up—support groups, counselors, transgender friends, doctors, the chat room online, the many websites that help us understand, the increasing volume of books and magazine articles and the many videos. Stuff we can share with others to help them accept our difference—to accept our real selves.

So we plan. We carefully plan with our friends and the seasoned transgendered persons from support groups, and those online. We do come out. We are going to survive. After all, we have survived the worst punishments of all—our own internalized punishments for not conforming to our culture's "socialization"—punishments that we saw or experienced, when we were little—the fears, the loneliness, the self-depreciation, and the keeping of the "secret." We have endured them all. We have survived the *internal* form of culturally induced stress and, thanks to those who came before us, we emerge into a world that is beginning to become more familiar with us and is more ready than ever to consider keeping us in the mainstream of culture.

SHARING OUR DECISIONS WITH OTHERS

When we come out, and announce to our world just who we really are, everyone is taken into a state of shock. Most people are kind, especially at first, while inside they must feel many emotions including panic and fear. We have announced that we are different, that we have successfully challenged culture's rules and "crossed the line." Once the announcement period is over, family, friends, coworkers, and everyone else in our world, appear to regain composure, and the cultural game of "resocialization" begins.

Their hope is to guide us into "changing back" to the sex that we were assigned at birth. Or if we do them both, that is, cross-dress, to hope that we will give up the "wrong" one. "It must be some phase," they say. We try and try to explain. They try and try to understand. But the rigid binary concept, taught so passionately, continues to exert its power within a short time after we give our facts to them. It seems so futile. Some family and friends stay with us. Others do not. We feel ourselves being pushed away from mainstream culture. People do not take us seriously. Some scoff at us. Others ignore us. Still others laugh at us, or make us wonder if they do. There is always that smile that seems to say—"We know. You are simply confused, dear."

More serious attempts develop to force us to "see the light." Discrimination introduces us to the worst in human behavior and leaves us filled with primitive rage. Then we get used to it. We know what it is like to be different and to have people—stupid, narrow-minded, ignorant people—judge us, as if they were so perfect. We become wiser to the truth of "culture"— savvier. We learn to rise above.

Everything we do, every change we decide to make, comes with the need to be careful, to get the facts, to find out how others did when they did the same thing before us. Name change, health care, legal representation, housing, employment, and other resources that are so freely available to others, require us to be more careful, more selective, to assure success.

Some of us become advocates for civil and human rights, or support our advocates with money and volunteer our time. Our advocacy will continually challenge culture to change—to include us—to protect us from the destructiveness of discrimination—and to see that different is not only beautiful, but it is the miracle of human diversity that makes it possible for human beings to survive, to create something new, to do so many things that make the world a better place.

We have experienced internal CIS, and we will always deal with the fear of retribution that we learned so long ago, as little ones. Now and always we will confront the *external* form of CIS. But we will survive—we will help others survive—and whenever we see any other people who are different by color, race, sex, age, or anyone else who is seen as different, we will sense a bond develop, for we know that the culturally induced stress that they experience brings us to share a common ground.

WHERE DO WE GO FROM HERE?

We press on. Within our community, we must free ourselves from judging one another; we must find common ground and support each other in ways that celebrate our *entire* transgender community—the entire continuum of transgender.

We must begin to gather data. As culture becomes more open and accepting of us, or perhaps more correctly, less oppositional to us, more transgendered people will come out. We must help them make this courageous stand successfully. Data will allow us to identify our issues, our needs, and our contributions. Data collection is very possible. Gender-Pac did it in 1997 and the Human Rights Commission did it in 2002. We must continue efforts to get on the cultural map. We must be on the cultural radar. We must be part of the state and national census. Otherwise we are statistically nonexistent.

We must help create an environment that enables transgendered persons to come out safely at an earlier age. Then, the possibility of a full and happy life can be realized.

We must never give up. We must educate, educate, educate. We must advocate, advocate, advocate. Persistence is the only way to move the cultural paradigm.

HOW CAN YOU HELP?

As counselors/therapists: Be open to learning the truth about transgender—that it is not a psychiatric disorder, but a physical issue that has not been understood until research, reported in recent years, identified the site of sex identity—which is the brain. This means that you will need to *un*learn your own socialization, which told you that the genitals define sex identity. They do not.

Become aware of your own comfort levels. Some helpers just are not appropriate to work with the transgender community, just as some cannot work with excessively dependent people or with spousal abusers.

Become aware of the Standards of Care established by the Harry Benjamin International Gender Dysphoria Association, Inc. Are you qualified to work with transgendered persons?

Become aware of the transgender community and of the resources available in that community.

Be prepared to provide *supportive* counseling to transgendered persons, which could also include family work, employment advocacy, and working with medical persons.

In understanding the physical etiology of transgender—the brain—and in understanding that the brain's "will" is even stronger than the rigors of cultural socialization, it must follow that the idea of "reparative therapy" (brainwashing) is not only inappropriate but is harmful to the transgendered person over time.

As family or friends: Learn all you can about transgender. You too have a journey to travel in dealing with your intense feelings regarding your transgendered family member or friend. Don't abandon the transgendered person. He or she can help you adjust by giving you information. The transgendered person has already journeyed far and knows a good deal about your struggle—for he or she has struggled with most of the same things that you are struggling with.

As coworkers: Learn all you can. Don't be afraid to ask questions; ask them. Remember, everyone is there to do a job. Sex identity should never render someone less competent. The transgendered worker has gone through what most will never experience. It has left the "new" person far stronger than most people.

Don't push the bathroom issue. It is the most foolish issue that culture has ever come up with to say it doesn't like adjusting to the transgendered person. If a worker has an "issue" with the transgendered person using the bathroom appropriate to his or her "new" sex and gender, then let that worker find another place to go. Forcing the transgendered person to make an accommodation is the same thing as saying that the transgendered person is the worker with the problem, when if fact, he or she is not the one with the problem at all.

Generally, as people in the culture:

1. Be kind to transgendered people, now that you know the truth.

2. When you see a transperson, smile. That individual needs extra reassurance to overcome the fear that you would reject him/her.

3. Use the pronoun appropriate to the person's clothing and appearance. If you are not sure, respectfully ask the transperson how he/she wants to be addressed.

4. Correct others who make unkind remarks about transgendered persons.

5. Help transpersons feel accepted on the job or in educational settings.

6. Support transpersons' efforts at obtaining legal protection from discrimination, by adding "gender or gender expression," or other suitable language, to antidiscrimination laws.

7. Support transpersons in having health insurance carriers include, *not* exclude, transgendered people in their health care covered services, as a medically necessary condition.

8. Invite a transperson to your club, association, or group meeting to learn more about transgender.

9. Welcome transpersons in your church or faith community and encourage them to join.

10. Tell someone you know about what you have learned about transgendered people.

3

THE ALLY'S JOURNEY

Anne L. Boedecker, ph.d.

A TRANSGENDER ALLY IS ANYONE who openly supports and affirms trans-sexuals, cross-dressers, androgynes, bigendered and transgendered peo-ple. The stories in this book are about transformation—stories of how people discover, come to terms with, and embark on a journey of explo-ration, affirmation, and expression of their gendered self. Many of them write about losing and gaining people in their lives due to that transfor-mation. The people who stay with them or befriend them along the way are also transformed by their experience. I've been asked to write about what I have learned from working with transgender clients in my psy-chology practice, and from my experience with a family member's gen-der exploration. My own personal and professional journey is ongoing, with more changes and challenges ahead, I'm sure. This is simply a re-flection at this point in time on the process of becoming an ally and what this work means to me.

So what does it take to become an ally? At the most basic level all it takes is an open mind and an open heart—the ability to see and appreciate another human being underneath layers of social roles. It requires the same open mind and open heart that it takes to be supportive and affirming of any type of diversity—the ability to free our mind of stereotypes, to listen and let someone's story unfold, to try and understand and appreciate differences, and to respect the basic right of self-determination. It also requires the willingness to examine our own beliefs and assumptions about gender and gendered behavior, and to be able to see gender as more complex and fluid than simply born male or female. Beyond that, it simply takes the willingness to learn.

I first began seeing transgender folk when a referral service was looking for someone with knowledge of sex and gender development to work with a transgender client. I had enough academic background, and curiosity, to give it a try. That first client was so convincing as a man that I wasn't sure at first if he was really a female-to-male transsexual or a male-to-female! I knew right away that I had a lot to learn. Fortunately, the client brought with him a reading list and a copy of the Harry Benjamin Standards of Care. The more I read the more intrigued I became with the diversity of gender variance. Every transgender story is unique, and each can be as heart-warming as it is heart-wrenching. And the more gender variant people I saw as clients and met outside the office the more I wanted to help.

Yes, these people come to me in a lot of pain and with a lot of problems. They have had to cope with a tremendous burden of shame and secrecy in their lives, and more than their share of alienation and rejection. It is heart-wrenching at times to listen to all the struggles they've been through, and the intensity of their gender dysphoria. But I am impressed by the courage these clients show in coming to me and opening up to a stranger. Many have been mistreated by mental health professionals before. Their appreciation for the understanding, acceptance, and encouragement I offer them is definitely heart-warming. Their motivation and commitment to the process of change, no matter how much they have to sacrifice, is inspiring. I feel blessed to be able to support them on their journeys. I have learned a great deal from them, not only about gender and human nature, but also about myself.

Not everyone becomes an ally by choice, of course. For most, it starts with someone they know sitting them down, or sending a letter, often with photos, to tell that person's story. The transgender person is full of hopes and fears, knowing that reactions can vary from extremely negative to fairly positive. And people's reactions to a gender change do vary, and vacillate—from "It's about time!" to "Are you out of your mind?" My transgender clients have been surprised at how supportive people can be. One of the most common responses is "Whatever makes you happy . . . and you do seem happier." They are also often surprised at how difficult it is for close family members and significant others to accept the changes. It seems that the people closest to the transgender person have the most invested in the social role that he or she has been filling. Mothers and fathers, sisters and brothers, and certainly spouses, have the most to lose. Accepting that dramatic a change in someone they love involves a process of grieving and letting go of the old relationship in order to develop a new one.

So I will admit that when a member of my own family came to me asking for support on her transgender journey I wasn't as supportive as I could have been. My reactions were due in part to the particulars of the situations—the age of the person, and what I knew of her upbringing. But they were also driven in part by my own personal investment in how I saw her. I recognized in myself the stages of grieving, just as I saw them in the stories of others. I reacted first with shock and denial: "this can't really be happening!" I echoed so many others's thoughts: "this must be a stage," and "maybe it's the influence of the person she's seeing." I protested: "but she's such a beautiful young woman!" I felt insulted: "what's wrong with being a woman? I'm strong and assertive and competent and aren't I a woman?" I argued: "what's wrong with being a lesbian?" I bargained: "Please wait; talk to more people first." I feared for her safety. I despaired losing my relationship with the girl I knew. I struggled with what I should or shouldn't do, to try to slow her down and make her think more about what she was getting herself into. Then I realized I really couldn't do anything except continue to love her and support her as best I could. I let go of any control I thought I could have (but I kept my right to my own opinion). This has allowed us to continue to stay connected while we both sort out our feelings and adjust to our changing relationship.

I'm sure many allies go through a similar process. Some family members and significant others get stuck in denial, or anger, or despair. Some can't accept the changes, and lose their relationship as the person's journey goes on without them. Some wives keep trying to bargain and control, trying to limit their husband's dressing habits. Others can accept the changes, at least in theory, but decide they don't want to be in what would become a lesbian relationship. And a lesbian in a relationship with a female-becoming-a-man may decide that just won't work for her. They all have the opportunity to become a friend and ally, but their own hurt and anger often gets in the way. Those who stay connected are very courageous and in need of support from others as well. Those who accompany the transgender person on his or her journey share the pain, the fear, the hurt, the social ostracism, and the high emotional cost of leading a closeted or marginalized life. There are high economic costs as well, since hormone therapy and gender reassignment surgeries are not generally covered by insurance. Being in a relationship with someone undertaking the complete transition requires sacrifices on many levels.

So it often falls to therapists, gay, lesbian, bisexual, transgender activists, old and new friends, and other caring people to provide the support gender variant people need. Pastors, ministers, rabbis, and other spiritual leaders can fill a very important role. Transgender folk have most often been alienated from, or rejected by, the church they grew up in. Yet many seek spiritual guidance, and acceptance, from church and clergy. I have several clients who have been well supported by their faith communities. One woman had church members bringing her meals every day while she was recuperating from her surgery. Another first came out to her church, and relied heavily on its support as she began her transition.

You may be reading this because someone has come out to you, or in anticipation of ministering to transgender clients or parishioners. I hope you can appreciate the trust someone places in you when they reveal to you their true self. Transgender people are very cautious about whom they come out to, often researching carefully and checking with others before approaching someone for help. They bring all their hopes and fears to every encounter. Yet you can't expect yourself to be perfectly adept at handling your first meeting with someone so different from how we've been taught to see gender. It's OK to admit your limitations—in fact, it's imperative that you recognize and acknowledge them. It's the willingness to learn and outgrow those limitations that distinguishes an ally.

So how do you become an ally? How do you help the transgender client or parishioner or family member? You start by affirming your relationship with that person, and your care and concern. Then you listen and learn! Although it's important to listen to each person's unique story, it's not fair to rely on him or her to educate you about all the issues. *True Selves* by Mildred Brown and Chloe Ann Rounsley is a very good place to start. Internet resources are also valuable, for you and for the transgender client or parishioner. Your state or local PFLAG (Parents and Friends of Lesbians and Gays) chapter will most likely have information available, as well as any religious denomination that has an Open and Affirming or Welcoming Congregation program. If you live near a college or university, look for professors who teach courses in Gender Studies or Human Sexuality (but don't be surprised if their experience is limited), or for campus GBLT groups. Resources may be difficult to find at first, but once you tap into the culture, you'll be amazed at how much is out there.

Once you start reading and listening, you'll probably be surprised by how prevalent gender variance is. But the more you learn about the biology and psychology of the development of gender, the more transgender conditions will make perfect sense. And the more transgender folks you meet, the more amazed you'll be at how malleable external gender appearance can be. I have seen biological males transformed into attractive, poised, radiant women, in the space of a year. And I've met men who were born female whom no one would ever guess hadn't been male all their lives.

After affirming your relationship with a transgender person who has come out to you, there are a few simple questions that will help orient you. First of all, if you're confused about the direction of a person's transition, don't be afraid to ask. (The transgender person's "real" gender is the one the person is in the process of becoming, or has become. His or her "biological sex" is the one he or she was born with, or at least assigned at birth.) You can ask where the person is in the transition (and look up the terms later if that gets you more confused). Do ask how he or she would like to be addressed—name, pronouns—and how he or she would like to dress at your office, or church, or home. And be sure to ask how "out" the individual is, and respect his or her right to control who knows and who doesn't. *Never* disclose someone's TG status without his or her permission, or assume that someone is out to everyone, even if he or she seems open about it.

You will in all likelihood have your own reactions and opinions about a particular person's story. You may wonder how the balding male sitting before you can ever hope to pass as a woman. (You'd be surprised at how well hormones, the right clothes, make-up, and a wig can transform a toad into a princess.) Or you may worry about how this woman's children will cope with her transition to a man. (They do grieve the loss, but most children do just fine. What matters most is happy, loving parents.) It's important to find a place to process these reactions—with a knowledgeable friend or colleague, perhaps, or a therapist if necessary. Most transgender folk have enough to deal with; they don't need to be burdened with our fears or doubts or insecurities. Some will be secure enough to process these with you and guide you in coming to terms with their changes. Many have struggled with so much shame and guilt and insecurity that one more person's doubt or hesitancy can squash their openness. They don't always realize that just as they have had to take time to come to terms with their true nature, other people will need time to adjust too. If someone has trusted you with this disclosure, your support means a lot to him or her. Consider it a sacred moment, and a sacred trust.

This is beginning to sound like a lot of work, and sometimes it is. But the rewards are plentiful. One of the most universal is the personal growth that comes from examining one's own gender complexity. The transgender revolution picks up where the women's and men's movements of the sixties and seventies and the gay and lesbian movement of the eighties and nineties leave off. My generation of women rebelled against the rigidity of what social scientists called sex-role stereotypes. We argued that we should not be limited to proscribed roles and occupations because of being born female. Women reclaimed their right to self-determination, on many levels. Men reclaimed their right to have their own personal needs and feelings. Gays and lesbians have worked for the right to love whomever they love, without fear of violence and discrimination. Each movement has challenged restrictions based on gender, but still assumes that gender, and sexuality, are binary and fixed. The basic assumption is that you're born either male or female, gay or straight. Bisexuals and the transgender movement challenge the binary concept of sexuality and gender. They force us to look at something about ourselves that we take for granted, and examine it more closely. Am I as gay or straight as I think I am? Am I "100 percent male" or "all woman"? The richness and freedom that this exploration opens up is tremendous. We discover that we don't need to be defined by our gender-roles, psychologically and spiritually. In fact, we don't have to be defined by our gender at all. (Socially is another story, but that's the next challenge for twenty-first-century society.)

Another obvious reward is the growth in openness and acceptance that occurs. Many pastors and counselors have written about the blessing of accepting and welcoming gays and lesbians into their congregations and practices. Embracing diversity enriches our lives, allowing us to get to know people whose stories inspire us and touch our hearts. The transgender folks I know are for the most part wonderful people—warm and funny and down-to-earth. Their trials and tribulations have given them particular strengths, as well as psychological and spiritual insights beyond the ordinary. They are a pleasure to get to know. And in being more open and accepting with them, I find myself more accepting of other people who present themselves differently.

The most difficult benefit to describe is the often sacred intimacy that can develop between an ally and the person or people he or she supports. Stripped of the social norms and customs of relating to someone based on his or her apparent gender, we have no choice but to deal with this person as simply a unique human being, unable to be neatly categorized. Proper pronouns become useless artifacts of a language that cannot begin to capture someone's essential nature. Transgender in this case translates as transcending gender, and transcending conceptual barriers that separate *him* from *her, us* from *them*. It becomes an I-Thou relationship.

I hope this prepares you, in some way, to open your mind and heart as you read the stories in this book and encounter transgender people in your church, neighborhood, or workplace. But beware! To do so will invite a personal journey that just might get you involved in something bigger than yourself.

4

ONE PASTOR'S EXPERIENCE

DAVID TRAVERS

As I GREETED THE CONGREGATION that morning in preparation for leading the call to worship, my attention was quickly drawn to the well-dressed woman who slipped in quietly at the last minute, and who would leave rather hurriedly after the service. I had known that she'd appear sooner or later; what I wasn't prepared for was that she'd be wearing clothes I'd seen my wife wear dozens of times.

Sixty or so other folks noticed her as well. Those few in whom she had previously confided were relieved at her appearance; most were surprised or startled or curious or confused or simply indifferent; one or two were at least mildly distressed. The congregation already had to deal with a rather flamboyant cross-dresser for a couple of months each year; was this to be another test of tolerance?

So began the new church life of a well-loved, long-time member of the only church in this small, quiet town in northern New England. Zinny had lived for a couple of decades in a tiny village at the west end of the town, where the local station and the long-abandoned grade of the rail line from the state's capital to its western border reminded one of bygone, if not simpler, days. Since emigrating from Latvia as a young boy, his gentle spirit and inquisitive mind led him to develop skills in carpentry and woodworking, in music and photography and amateur radio, in motorcycling and automotive mechanics. He had fathered two sons, and seemed to have enjoyed a traditional family life with no major calamities. His Baptist upbringing had kept him involved in the church, where he sang in the choir and frequently offered vocal and instrumental music with a small group of other musicians. Warm, friendly, and eager to help, he was a beloved asset to both church and community.

We seemed to develop a trusting relationship rather quickly, and within a few weeks of my arrival as the church's interim pastor he asked for a block of my time so he could share what was *really* going on in his life. He told me of having returned to school a few years ago. In the process he found the courage to explore what had become an increasingly nagging sense that his was a woman's being encased in a man's body and cultural expectation. His/her concerns centered on the need to share this newfound conviction with family, friends, church, and workplace. She seemed quite secure and at ease with both her own sexuality and her faith, and she needed both to talk about these things and to understand how I responded to it all.

A local innkeeper deeply involved in the life of the congregation, the vivacious mother of an elementary-age boy, had taken her under her wing, tutoring her in all manner of womanly things. The warmth and joy of that relationship did much to prepare her and (perhaps at the time unknowingly) the congregation for the road ahead. My wife, Nan, was soon brought into the gradually growing group of those who knew. The first of their many shopping trips was to Nan's own clothes closet!

It is, of course, perfectly normal that pastors keep a great many confidences about their parishioners' lives, and learn to function accordingly. Most of those secrets are just that; they are no one else's business, and the goal is to keep it that way. The purpose here was quite different; an awesome discovery was radically transforming one person's life and would eventually affect every other life connected with it. This news simply *had* to be shared, and some hearers might need to be supported as they processed it and adjusted to a new reality. The pastoral opportunities would unfold rapidly, and I knew instinctively that many would take their cues from my own attitudes and behaviors. I wanted to find that balance point between taking the situation seriously without making it into a problem to be solved and taking it in stride without trivializing or being patronizing. I had never walked with someone through the transgendering process before, nor had I ever guided a congregation through such a time. I felt empty, but called to stand up and do something.

So I did what introverts always do in such situations. I browsed through my heart and soul, mind and guts, and whatever else I could find inside, finding bits of memory and feeling and imagery and insight and perspective and inspiration that kept opening me up for more and more. My strong background in Jungian psychology provided both conceptual framework and empathic connection for shaping responses. Initial anxieties were quickly replaced by an almost mystical sense of life manifesting itself profoundly, of spirit joining substance, of wholeness and holiness happening right here in our midst. And it seemed that rather than fight battles or try to change anyone's mind or behavior, all I had to do was be there and help people see what was happening—and if some didn't, that wasn't really my problem.

Although odd little things during this time of gestation would give me pause to think them through, I must say that the most difficult thing for me was to make the conceptual and linguistic shifts from masculine to feminine gender (although this seems a bit silly now in retrospect). Amber's affirmation of the English translation of her given Latvian name was of considerable help in my own process, but I had to concentrate on using the right pronouns and images, depending on whom I was with. Of course, part of the trick was in keeping up with changes in her. For example, after dinner at our house one night the conversation turned to rearranging our basement, and before I knew it, she was down there muscling a freezer halfway across the floor with little help from me. Then a few months further into her hormone therapy she wistfully mentioned that she probably didn't have the muscle mass any longer to wrestle a thirty-four-foot ladder and climb around on the steeply pitched roof to help me with some antenna work, although she'd be glad to assist in some other way.

Being new to this church myself, I was unsure as to how it would react. After that memorable Sunday morning, Amber never went back to dressing for church as a man; perhaps the choir robe kept her from being in people's faces, thus giving them a chance to adjust to the new reality.

She quickly discovered she could hang around at coffee hour and be herself with more and more people, which of course built her confidence wonderfully. I watched people connect with her in their own way and time, and, although that went more smoothly for some than for others, I am not aware of any unpleasant incidents. A couple of people told me that having known her previously helped them work through their own uneasiness, and seeing Amber's own relief and happiness confirmed that it was all okay.

There are two more formal settings worthy of mention. The church council had its regular meeting very shortly after her church outing. There were all sorts of committee reports and discussions, and as the meeting was nearing its end I was asked if I had anything to bring. I simply asked "What about the elephant in the living room?" Some seemed not to know what I was talking about, even when told, while others caught on right away. What followed was about three-quarters of an hour of profound discussion of people's attitudes and feelings, their questions and commitments of support for both Amber (who was not present, and didn't know I was going to bring this up) and the church itself, and genuine concern for helping this transition go as smoothly as possible. It was wonderful to see people helping each other work through their responses, which ranged from "live and let live" to wondering about some sort of perversion to speculation that this was some sort of mid-life dalliance that would soon pass to compassion for a lifetime of pain and upcoming major adjustments. A similar experience was had at a diaconate meeting a couple of weeks later.

The only lasting negative response of which I am aware occurred when one of the key church school leaders proclaimed that Amber could do whatever she wanted with her life, but that she wasn't to get near "our" church school children. The rest of the committee firmly disagreed, and over time this person's position seems to have softened somewhat.

Perhaps the saddest part of this whole story concerns Amber's former wife. She, too, had been an active part of the church, particularly the church school. I suspect that she may have begun to drift away as the boys got older and became less involved. Church folk would try now and again to reach out to her, of course not knowing the struggles her husband's news was bringing her. By the time I arrived their divorce was well underway. I had a couple of brief contacts and one extended conversation with her, and could understand her feelings of betrayal and anger and confusion and near panic at having to start life over herself. There were simply too many reminders around the church of what happily had been and could no longer be, and the presence of this strange woman who had taken her husband away and toward whom she felt only fury. She could no longer see it as her church, as it became one more thing she lost. I felt shut out by her bitterness, and decided not to insist on maintaining a relationship with her.

This particular church has learned well (and practices often) how to pray and play together and care genuinely for one another; it can take almost anything in stride (including the painful dismissal of the previous pastor). In fact, that whole community displays an unusual acceptance of diversity and creativity, even while vigorously engaging the obligatory arguments over school budgets and maintenance of town roads! Wisely, Amber chose neither to take on the whole town at once, nor to strike out on her own to do her own thing. Her ability to know and explain herself and her own journey into wholeness produced a relatively small circle of strong support, and laid serious groundwork. Without this, the smooth transition for the rest of the church could not have happened. Her story is eloquent testimony to the power unleashed when one is faithful to what God calls one to be and shares that deeply with others. It reminds us that, given a chance, the creative forces of life and love will bear fruit beyond.

Part Two

IN OUR OWN VOICES

5

LIVING IN THE PALM OF GOD

DZINTRA ALKSNITIS

MY SPIRITUAL JOURNEY STARTED when I was a child. I grew up in a family that worshiped together regularly. I liked going to church and participating in the worship service. Early on I came to believe that if I asked God to come into my heart, my life would be better. The church taught me that I would have life everlasting. I believed then and I believe now.

What has changed over the course of my life is my understanding of who I am and how I relate to God. I have learned that God allows me to make decisions for myself. But I have also learned that there are consequences to all the decisions I make. I began to realize this after I had finally cornered myself.

Earlier in my life, while in denial, I had made decisions that now had serious consequences. I was closing in on fifty-one years of age and almost twenty years in a marriage that had given me wonderful gifts, including two now grown sons and many good years in a relationship with my wife.

At the time of my realization that something was very wrong I was finishing my junior year at college. I had returned to college to get a new start in life.

Little did I know that God had blessed my way to and through college not just because God wanted me to learn a new profession, but so that I could learn about the new me God planned to uncover.

One morning, April 4, 1999, on my fifty-five-mile commute to school, I realized that I could no longer live the way I had for the last forty years. I did not know what to do. I had become virtually inconsolable. Between tears and fears I went to class. I was taking several upper level courses, as is normal in a junior year. If I recall correctly there was University Physics III, Analytical Environmental Chemistry, a 300-level astronomy class, and Spanish 101 . . . my last general education class.

Nothing seemed to work, I could not focus on my studies, my mind wandered while I was in class, and I could not sleep. My home life seemed to be in shambles. I could not accomplish anything around the house because school was taking all my energy. The first two years in college I was able to work part time, not any more. There were expectations from the other members of my family, expectations I no longer could fulfill. I did not want to go to Sunday worship. It was too hard to listen to the morning message. I no longer wanted to participate in the choir. I loved singing in the choir and had done so for more than twenty years. I now found myself too emotional when the lyrics spoke to me, which happened most of the time. I had never felt like this before, helpless and scared.

My only way out was to find help. At first I did not know what to do. I could not tell my family that I was falling apart. I could not go to our health insurance because I would have to tell my wife what was wrong. At that time I did not know what was wrong and felt ashamed of feeling so powerless. I did not have money to go to an independent therapist and pay for it out of my pocket. On top of that I was afraid to go and seek help. I was afraid of what I might find.

I did not have a lot of confidence in myself, yet somehow I cried out to God for courage. The gifts I received I did not recognize. I found a way of getting help. I had tucked away in the front pocket of my notebook a flier from the counseling department. The flier had a whole list of things, and one of them was anxiety. I could certainly say that I felt anxious!

The first time I went to the third floor of Elliot Hall, to find the counseling department, I never got there. I chickened out at the second floor and went to the bathroom, shaking, to find my composure. The bathroom was occupied. I eventually found another bathroom on the first floor and wiped the fear from my face. It was time to try again, so up the steps I went the second time. This time I was successful in reaching the third floor. At the top of the steps was a framed directory of all the therapists who worked there. I was about to leave and go down the steps, telling myself that I'd better get to class, when a kind voice said to me, "Can I help you with something?"

That is how it began, the most challenging, scary, intimidating, and difficult journey of my life. The gifts I received as I had cried out to the Spirit were peace, understanding, love, courage, faith, and wisdom. Little did I know that I was going to need every one of these in order to survive and grow. When I cried out to the Spirit I did not know if the Spirit would actually answer my cry, I had not been in touch for a long time. I had been trying to do it all by myself.

My first visit to the therapist was the most difficult. I did not have a clear idea of what was wrong with me. To my surprise, when I was asked to describe how I felt and why I had sought help, out came the phrase "I think I need to be a woman." I can remember feeling dirty, perverted, immoral, scared, and very alone. At the same time I realized that I was not surprised at the words I had just uttered. When I looked across at my therapist I saw that she had not had any negative reaction to what I had just said. All she wanted to know is what else I felt and if I knew why. We talked about why I felt all the negative feelings about myself until I was able to resolve them.

God works through all kinds of people in order to help us heal. Although many of my caregivers are Christians, some are not. Throughout my journey I have been blessed by all their love and talent. Who am I to judge the people in my life who help me grow? This was my first lesson about God's love. God loves every one of us just as we are.

I continue to live in a small town in New Hampshire. I have been worshiping in the same church in the middle of town since 1980. Usually things change slowly in the life of a church.

I was faced with two major decisions. One was: should I move where I would have anonymity? And the other was: should I plan to worship in another church where I could start fresh? I decided not to make either change. My reasoning was that moving away meant that I had no support and no history. History is important. When people have known you for twenty years they are less likely to be judgmental of your personal choices. They know your character, they have observed your faith in God, and they know who you are. I certainly did not want to give up friends who had become my circle of angels.

Having chosen to stay, it was time to find the courage and start making the necessary changes in my daily life. This meant that I was going to start the visible part of my transition. I was so filled with fear that I could not reason with myself. I was afraid that just as my family had abandoned me, so would the community and I would become an outcast, an oddity, living in a small town.

I think that the hardest thing for me to do was to start worshiping as myself. I had been able to go out of my house dressed as a female for brief periods of time, but I was fearful of interacting with others. I was afraid that I did not have it all together. I could go to therapy as a female and if I were out with someone else I felt ok. To go to worship and put it all on the line just terrified me.

All things do come to pass, and my day to start worshiping as Amber was quickly approaching. The choir at church already knew something was up. I had a few friends there who knew the whole story. The whole church though . . . that was so huge.

I woke up early one Sunday morning in February 2001. I had made my favorite breakfast, and I was sitting in my chair journaling. As it had the last three Sundays, my mind went to pondering what I should wear to church today. For the first time in my life, there was a relentless feeling in my heart that I needed to worship as the person God had so magnificently created. Furthermore I felt that I needed to present myself truthfully before God in worship. I did not know quite what to do with these strong feelings. I was too scared to just go and do it. So I prayed that God would confirm it. I promised that if I found something to wear to church that I felt pretty in, I would take that as confirmation. I didn't think that there was a chance that this could happen.

God works in strange ways. About a month before that, a wonderfully supportive and loving friend had said to me "Amber, have you ever played dress up?" Of course my answer was no. We made a date to play dress up at her house. She explained that although we were different heights, she thought our body shapes and sizes were close enough that I might find some things I would like. She was cleaning out her wardrobe.

I came home with many outfits and singles that fit and looked very nice. I had dressed in appropriate clothes, and had not felt guilty. Furthermore I had moral support from someone who loved me and understood.

From that wonderful evening I was now trying to find something to wear to church, a dress or a top and a skirt, something that made me feel comfortable. After trying on what seemed like many outfits, I looked up into the full-length mirror on the closet door and found to my surprise that I was pretty.

Of course now I had a real dilemma. God had made good with that end of the bargain, now how about me? I can remember shaking as I pulled myself together. It was particularly hard doing the makeup because my hands shook. I prayed that I was doing the right thing.

By the time I arrived at church I was already late for the choir rehearsal, usually held right before the service. I walked up the back steps of the sanctuary, so that I did not have to parade down the entire length of the church. I walked around the altar, put my purse and my jacket down in the first pew, and turned around to go up to the choir loft. My heart sank to my feet; it felt like everyone was watching. As I went past the sopranos in the first row, my best friend whispered to me, "You'll be alright, Amber." And so I was, I was alright.

After the rehearsal the choir goes down to the robe closet. Wearing a robe during the worship service made it a little easier for me, but I realized that my nylons and pumps could still be seen by everyone. There was no place I could hide. The worship service went well and after the worship service everyone gathered for refreshments downstairs in Fellowship Hall. I contemplated just taking the robe, the cross, and the stole off and going out the side door. But my girlfriends and some of the choir members were there, encouraging me to stay for a while. They stayed with me while we had some coffee and cookies. I got a big kiss on the cheek from one of my friends as I headed for home.

As I write about it I can still feel how my heart pounded that day. You know, God was faithful. God helped me to do what was so necessary for me to do. When I got home after church I stayed dressed in my good clothes for a while. I felt wonderful about the whole experience. I had been true to myself and to God.

That experience has made a huge difference throughout the rest of my life. It was a leap of faith for me. I was blessed with enough courage to do what I needed to do. The friends who supported me in my first day of worship were friends with whom I had shared my journey. It was my new family given to me by God in order that I might grow in love.

This was the beginning of another chapter in my quest to be me. The church had a new challenge on their hands. No one had ever transitioned in this church as far as I knew. I can't really say how others felt about my intrusion into their orderly lives. I participated in Bible studies and church activities like I always had. I continue to sing in the choir. Slowly people learned that I was still pretty much the same person who had been worshipping in their midst since 1980.

The interim minister was very helpful, not only to me, but to other members of the congregation. He brought up the subject of my transition to the various committees as he attended their regular meetings. These small group discussions provided the committee members a more intimate space to talk about their feelings regarding my presence at worship. There have been no issues of intolerance or disrespect. Most people have warmed up to me over the course of the last twenty months. An interesting comment I have heard from some of my fellow parishioners is that they have discovered a new person in me, one who no longer is angry. I'm grateful.

One profound understanding is that all people minister to each other as they live their lives. My life is not just one sided, me taking the love from those around me in order to achieve my selfish goals and fulfill my personal needs. We all interact with each other as we live our lives and struggle with growth. Many people accept discrimination and prejudice as a part of their life. These feelings come from fear, fear of finding out that perhaps they themselves might be different. As people find out that I am a good person who loves the same things they love, they learn that there is diversity among God's children and that diversity is good. My walk in life is a ministry teaching others about tolerance and acceptance. I have observed changes in peoples' beliefs as they face the issues and work them out for themselves.

I mentioned earlier that professional counseling was God's gift of life to me. By April of 2001 I had been in therapy for two years. Most people transitioning have usually made up their minds by then. I was a slow poke. I was really ready to make some decisions, but was somewhat timid. My therapist encouraged me to sort out my feelings and find a direction for my transition. I had to decide if I was going to start on hormone therapy and let my body develop into the woman I longed to be, or was I going to stop here and be satisfied with where I was in my transition.

Hormone therapy can start off slowly if you so wish. I was not a young woman and so my hormone therapy started with an 81mg aspirin tablet daily. This was done so that I would not experience blood clot issues with the Premarin. The journey into hormones is so very personal and very special. I felt subtle changes initially My perfume began to smell different once I was on Premarin. My body developed a sweeter presence. I became much quieter and felt much less pushed to compete to be the "queen of the castle." My life became so much more manageable that I thought at first that I was just dreaming up these things trying to convince myself that I was on the right track. After two months of taking a low dose of Premarin we added an anti-antigen to start decreasing the effects of my testosterone production. To achieve normal blood levels for a woman, my doses have been systematically increased and balanced by my physician and my endocrinologist.

God has been in my life from the first day. Even the experiences of my body developing into a woman have felt like gifts. When I first looked in the mirror in April 1999 I saw a terrified, lonely, and ugly man staring back at me. There was nothing I could do about who I saw in the mirror. Subtly, my self-image has changed over the course of my transition. I see a pretty woman looking back at me now, someone who has a sparkle in her eye. That sparkle is God in my heart.

Over the last three and a half years, friends have included me in their observance of seasonal and religious holidays. Someone is always taking pictures to record the event. To my surprise, when I look at the pictures I can see changes happening. The changes in my appearance are not just changes in my mind's eye, they are actually noticeable physical changes. I am very pleased with the progress.

I gave this journey to God when I first started. I did it because I knew that I had to, not because I wanted to. I understood from past experience that if I did not give it to God, I would not experience all of God's blessings.

I was invited to my youngest son's wedding planned for late September of 2002. My son, his fiancé, and I had talked about the logistics and agreed on a plan back in June of 2002. We were dealing with conflicting interests. My son wanted me to be at his wedding as his dad. I wanted to go, but there was no way that I could go as a male. His army buddies were going to be there as the honor guard. Since no one within my son's circle of friends, both civilian and army, knew that I was transitioning, there was no real way that I could have been a part of the wedding. I had two remaining choices. I could not attend or I could go as a guest. It was a difficult way to go, but I chose to go as a guest. I was stripped of my identity, but at least I could see him get married.

I was hurt by the inability of my son to respect me as his parent and include me in the event. My son had not arrived at a place in his life where he could accept me for who I really am. Attending the wedding was emotionally painful and exhausting. I presented myself as an adult woman with lots of poise and a smile. Most of the family warmed up to me by the end of the day. There were three exceptions, my ex-wife, my ex-mother-in-law, and my brother's wife. When I went through the reception line my ex-wife would not look at me. She shook my hand and coldly said, "How do you do." My ex-mother-in-law refused to look at me or shake my hand. My brother's wife refused to look at me and interact with me in any way. I guess it is their loss.

Good things happened to me at the wedding reception as well. It became clear that my brother and his family were going to need a ride to the reception hall. Since I had room in my car, I was asked if I would give three of them a ride. I was happy to help. When we arrived I needed a little help to get the wedding present out of the back seat of the car. I asked my brother if he would get it out for me and he obliged. He then offered to carry it in for me and even held the door open so that I could enter first. I don't know if he intentionally treated me like a lady or if it just happened naturally. I enjoyed the respect.

Life continues to have its difficult times. Now that the wedding is over I have tried to stay in touch with the newlyweds. I have called and left several messages without receiving a reply. My oldest son, who did not go to the wedding, has not replied to my calls for months. So I worry about my adult children. I guess nothing has changed since their childhood. If they are yours you worry about them.

Two weeks after my son's wedding, my niece, who is also my godchild, was getting married. Initially I received an invitation from her. She asked that I come as her uncle. At my son's wedding it became clear to her that I would not be able to attend her wedding as her uncle. We talked about it at the wedding and my niece expressed her wish for me to come as I was. She just wanted me to be there. Less than a week later her invitation was revoked by my brother. If my sister-in-law was unable to interact with me at my son's wedding, then why would she be able to do so at her daughter's wedding?

It was not long after this last family celebration, my niece's wedding, that I looked at all the events my biological family had in 2002. There were weddings, college graduations, Easter celebrations, and many more. It seems clear that my family is no longer welcoming my presence in their lives, and I find it painful. I often find it difficult not to consider my biological family's behavior as abandonment.

The latest e-mails between my brother and I have been a continuation of the previous discussions we have had over the last three years. He wants me to stop transitioning, seek a Christian therapist, and return to my previous male status. Since I have refused to honor his wishes our interactions have become difficult. This year my biological family has asked me not to come to the traditional Christmas Eve celebration. They want me to come for a visit after the holidays, but only if I come dressed as a male. Nothing has changed.

I have chosen to disassociate myself with my family. I wrote them a letter describing my feelings and expressing my hopes that maybe sometime in the years to come we all might experience sufficient healing to be able to come together and function as a family again. In the meantime I have planned to spend the holidays with friends nearby who want me and have invited me to become a part of their family.

We can't always stay in the family relationship we were born into. This is particularly true if that relationship is tearing us apart. Our biological families cannot always accept us and support us the way we need to be supported as we transition. Some people just don't understand and can't find a way of accepting us. This does not mean that they do not love us. I know that at first I was really hurt that my family could not fulfill my expectations of them. The other side of the coin is that I could not fulfill their expectations of me as well.

It would only be fair to say that not everything turns out badly. My experiences with my family have been the most painful of all. There are many positive things that have happened in the three and a half years that I have been transitioning.

My life has been blessed richly because I let Jesus in my heart a long time ago. I have successfully been living in role now for more than a year. I still worship at my home church, I sing in the choir, and I am loved by most of the people in my church. I am active in two committees, the music committee, and the pastoral relations committee. My life has blossomed as I let God work through me.

I have been playing in a secular music group for the last two years. From time to time we perform on stage at various venues. At present we are all writing original music and working on arranging our songs. We have recorded a demo CD and hope to have a complete CD of our work ready to sell in the spring. It is fun hearing one's own creations come to life. I experience new challenges as I sing and play our music. As I become proficient in playing other instruments I look forward to bringing them into the group. It is a safe place to express what is in my heart.

There is still a lot of unfinished business challenging me. I have learned a lot living in role. It really is not living in role anymore. I just live my life as an adult woman. Life is full of subtle changes that take their place as I live each day.

6

I AM DIFFERENT!!

P AMELA R EED

I am different.

Why?? Because I choose to be who I am not what society dictates!
Men think I have chosen to become a second class citizen.
Women applaud my courage in understanding my trueself!
What is this difference??
I have admitted to myself that I am female not male as the doctors
declared when I was born.
They chose based on some external visual objects. I chose because in my
heart I have always known!!
I tried their way and it led to despair and darkness!!

THEN I CHOSE LIFE!!!

7

TERRY'S JOURNEY

TERRY DRESSER

I'M TERRY, a thirty-two-year-old female-to-male transsexual. I've known since I was five years old that I was supposed to be a boy. It was a feeling deep down inside that I was really a boy instead of girl. I was lucky in a lot of ways because my mother allowed me to be as much of a tomboy as I wanted, with few restrictions. It wasn't until puberty that I really had to start dealing with the expectations society had for me because of being born into a female body. I had people telling me how to dress and how to act. I also had to deal with my body developing into a something that didn't feel natural. I struggled every morning, waking to find a female body after dreaming of being fully male. Some mornings I would cry and become angry at the contradiction my body presented. I started self-mutilating my chest in anger. I tore at my chest daily, hating the lumps that were quickly growing into breasts.

When I was seventeen, I started to learn about gays and lesbians. A local TV show for teens discussed the subject. I was asked if I was a lesbian by a teacher, a therapist, and a social worker. From their questions, and from the teen show, I felt that lesbians were at least accepted for the most part. I started to think that maybe I was a lesbian instead of a boy.

At one point I ended up in a psychiatric hospital for a month. In the hospital, they tried to get me to be more comfortable with being female. I was forced to wear women's clothing and makeup every day. I was forced to act, walk, and talk like a professional woman. I was also forced to go outside the unit and walk the hospital grounds every day with a supervisor to make sure I was always acting and speaking correctly. To get out of the hospital, I had to say I was comfortable being a woman.

After I left the hospital, I tried to keep up a feminine appearance at least when I went to work. But my employer at the time complained I was not feminine enough. And a relationship I was in during that time did not work because, no matter how hard I tried to find my feminine side, it wasn't enough for my girlfriend and the relationship ended.

At twenty-nine, I went on disability due to a diagnosis of bipolar disorder. I started taking a serious look at my life: my friends, my attitude, and who and what I was. I slowly started to weed out the true friends from the ones who were not good for me. Finally one day, after a night of dreaming as a man, I woke up and looked at my body and realized I could no longer take the lie of my life any longer. It was time to accept who and what I was: a transsexual.

After talking with many close friends, I started my transition: got rid of all female clothing, purchased more men's clothing, took the psychological test, started taking male hormone injections, bound my chest, and changed my name. After a few months on the hormones I started noticing remarkable changes, especially in my bipolar disorder. Before the hormones, I was taking the maximum of six medications but was still not very stable. After the hormones, I was able to drop to three. I am now more stable then I have ever been before.

I went through a difficult time of losing friends, losing my church family, confusing people out in public, and actually having to show identification to use a bathroom in a bar one night. Several nights I would go home and cry from the frustration of trying to be me in a society that does not accept differences. Finally, because of the changes the hormones made to me physically (facial hair, larger neck, lower voice, and broader shoulders) and having chest surgery, I started looking and sounding more like the man I am and was less likely to be confused as a female. I was lucky to find acceptance from my birth family.

The hardest part of my spiritual journey through this was losing a church that had felt like home for over ten years. They were not able to accept my transition. The church was mostly made up of gays and lesbians and that community sometimes seems to have a harder time with "trans" than the straight community does. I've been lucky to have a close relationship with God and to know deep down inside that no matter what others said I knew God loved me and accepted me as the child God created me to be. And I am so glad to have a found a church home where I can be myself and be accepted and loved.

8

BECOMING MORE AND MORE MYSELF[1]

BRAN SCOTT

I ALWAYS TELL PEOPLE I knew to whom I was attracted decades before I really knew who I was. I believe that's an experience not isolated to the transgendered. It is much easier to define one's self in relationship to those outside the self—I am more like Mom, less like my friend Jill, look like my dad, want to hold hands with the girl next door. Sex, gender, is much like God—we believe it is out there, we talk about it, we feel it deeply, and yet, in this life, we cannot get to it without looking through the lens of our own experience. We never experience either objectively. When we try to divide the world into two sexes, or three, or any set number, we must inevitably grapple with the fact that human beings are not easily divided into categories. We have far more similarities than we do differences, and our statistical averages expose our cultural assumptions to embarrassing mathematical problems. If, according to statistics reported by the Intersexed Society of North America, one or two in a thousand children are born with genitals that are surgically altered to conform to our cultural norms, as the generations multiply, can we still really claim that human beings arrive in only two sexes? Is a man who loses his penis to cancer still a man? Is a woman who does not use her uterus to bear children still a woman? But yet, sex is there, somewhere; we can feel it, we live with it, we understand our bodies through it. It is comforting short-hand in our daily lives.

I was born a transperson in 1970, to an educated middle-class family in the South. I was perceived to be female, and although I knew I was different in some way, I had no language to talk about that difference. As I grew into the era of '70s feminism, I was assured that my feelings of difference were not really about sex, but were about our cultural roles. I was assured that girls could do anything boys could. I played soccer on the all-boy team, liked math, had short hair, carved wood, dressed in jeans and t-shirts, and (until puberty) had mostly male friends, all with the full support of my parents. I was also terribly shy, liked poetry and reading, and hated competition and conflict. In the era when the deep truths of women's power, equality, and freedom were finally breaking open our closed society, my struggles to fit in and to find myself were seen by my parents and mentors to be a smaller part of the larger struggle for women's rights to self-determination.

Although my issues were slightly different, I was blessed to learn from those feminists, civil rights leaders, and lesbian and gay heroes who paved the way for my fuller self-exploration and questioning of cultural norms. At an early age, I also realized that I liked girls. Yes, I liked girls, in that way. Attraction was clear to me, that chemical reaction of sights, sounds, smells, and mystery that lures one through the door of adolescence. I came out as a lesbian at sixteen and thought that being queer explained all the nagging not-fitting-in, body discomfort, not-being-myself.

But it didn't. I never grew out of that awkwardness, or the nagging, persistent, depressing feelings of being out-of-place. I did grow successfully into high school, then college. On the way I encountered a loving Christian community to replace the hateful, homo- and difference-phobic Christianity I encountered as a young queer person in Arkansas. I became a Christian in 1994, in my first year out of college, dedicating my life to being a disciple of Jesus Christ. I entered seminary. And, in my first year of seminary, I encountered my first female-to-male transsexual. Or, I should say, I encountered my first image of a female-to-male transsexual.

Trans-bodies are beautiful bodies. Look closely at our faces, our hands, our chests, our hips, our whole physical beings, for we, too, are people God created. Our hands have worked in fields, written manuscripts and code, raised children, and molded beautiful lives in a difficult world. Our faces show pride, wisdom, courage, love, and, yes, pain. Our bodies, complete now in any alterations we have chosen, were known when we were still in our mothers' wombs. My first image of a female-to- male transsexual was photographer Loren Cameron's "Gods Will." It is an amazing black-and-white self-portrait of Cameron, bearded, tattooed, muscular, flexing, naked, and injecting himself with testosterone. I saw that picture on the front page of the San Francisco *Bay Guardian* in my third year of seminary and said to myself, I want to look like that.

And when I stopped running, some months later, I picked up and read the article. I read more and more, both theoretical and practical works about transpeople, and began to talk with people. My life began to break open, making sense, deep sense, for the first time. I not only knew who I was but had found language to express that reality, and language to share with others in conversation.

My decision to transition came as a second step. I knew then that I was a transgendered person. The question was: What should I do about it? I saw two paths: I could transition physically, socially, and legally, and face possible discrimination, hatred, and violence in a new physical and cultural reality, or I could remain female-bodied, present as female in the world, and be closeted about my transgender status. I began to pray. I prayed that God would tell me whether God wanted me to transition or not. I prayed and prayed, listened and listened, and began to know that God didn't care. God didn't care whether I transitioned or not, because God knew me as I was, had been, and would be. In the freedom of that knowledge, I began a new prayer. I prayed to God to know which path would lead me to be the fullest, best person I could be, to serve God and others the best I could. I decided to begin transition in 1997, in my last year at seminary, starting hormones and having chest surgery, changing driver's license and legal name, coming out to family, friends, professors, and my school.

Since that time, I have become more and more myself. I am finally comfortable in my own skin, with all its quirks and beauties, more comfortable speaking in public, in taking risks, in reaching out to others, in just being. I am blessed with a supportive family and wife. I have also been blessed to have been able to direct my own transition and care, to be the decider and achiever of my life as a transsexual man. I owe this blessing to the many transpeople who went before me, who refused to be seen as diseased or perverted, who fought battles against medical, legal, and social discrimination for rights as simple as the right to author one's own physical being, the right to parent children, the right to hold employment, gain housing, or use a public restroom. The right to have the grotesque murders of people like us, far too many in the past years, counted as tragedies rather than inevitabilities.

I have faced some barriers since transition—the withdrawal of job offers, the loss of some friends and family, the fear of persecution. I still think sometimes about how my life would have been had I been born biologically male. But for all the advantages of being born with body, mind, spirit, and cultural expectations wrapped into a tidy and unassuming package, I would, simply, not be the person I am today, the person I believe I was in fact meant to be, and the person God has intended in me. My prayers these days are simple. I pray to grow in God's love, and point to God's love in the world. To help someone else know that he or she, too, is loved by God and can become the person God intends. To be the best man I can be.

NOTES

1. From *Transgender Pocket,* copyright © 2000, the UCC Coalition for Lesbian, Gay, Bisexual, and Transgender Concerns. Used by permission.

9

LOVE IS TENDER AND KNOWS NO GENDER

ROSE A.

I'M NOT SURE HOW TO DESCRIBE our "rainbow" family, especially in conventional terms, but I'll try to start on common ground. My husband was born intersexed, raised as a female, married, and transitioned back to male after raising several children. His daughter is in a Christian committed lesbian relationship; his sons appear to be heterosexual. I've self-identified as bisexual and androgynous for as long as I can remember. My daughter came out as a lesbian as a teen and does her best to challenge traditional notions of sex and gender. Our faiths and faith communities have been an integral part of all of our personal journeys, providing support, inspiration, and a strong sense of purpose and meaning. Our experiences with sexuality and gender have had a profound impact on our spiritual growth as well.

J was born in a military hospital, to first generation Americans. His mother had been ill during the pregnancy. He was born with ambiguous genitalia and mixed reproductive organs. Like many others born that way, he was surgically altered and presented to his parents as a girl. His family knew J was different from his sisters, and in their own way let him be himself. He felt free as a child because gender wasn't an issue. He was allowed to be artistic and expressive as well as active and adventurous. He hated dresses and "girl toys," preferring to spend time playing outside or with his father. He remembers the males in his life—his father and uncle, and especially his pastor—as gentle, compassionate men. His father was a minister and social activist, and an influential role model. His spirituality evolved around his love of nature and an image of Christ as a wonderful teacher who loved children. He had a spontaneous prayer life and a trusting relationship with "God the father." He felt his spirituality and creativity was supported by his church, at least until a new pastor arrived when he was fourteen.

Around the same time, his parents became concerned because J showed no signs of normal female development. J was just disappointed that his friends were now becoming more gender-conscious and didn't consider him "one of the boys" anymore. He became self-conscious, and withdrew into himself. "She" was sent to a specialist at age sixteen. The exam was traumatic, but only the beginning of a medical maltreatment that lasted twenty years. The doctor was insensitive to "her" feelings, and ignorant about "her" condition. The only thing the doctor knew how to do was prescribe increasing amounts of estrogen. The ensuing emotional upheavals and bodily changes left J feeling confused and inadequate. He describes it as "walking into hell," wearing a body that didn't fit. He lost himself, trying to figure out who/how to be from other people's expectations of the woman he was supposed to be. He lost a lot of trust in doctors. J also lost his trusting relationship with God.

In J's attempts to adjust, s/he married early, and sought refuge in a conventional role of wife and mother. S/he worked until having children, and then became very involved in all of their activities. Being with kids provided some meaning and value in a life that didn't feel quite right, as well as an outlet for his/her creativity. J's husband was more of a buddy than a true partner, and certainly did not meet any sexual or spiritual needs. Being part of a family was important to them both, however, and kept them together for fifteen years. J brought his/her family to different Christian churches at different times, looking for a spiritual community. He describes it as looking for a conventional "God in a box." S/he never felt quite at home in any of them, or anywhere else for that matter. Not being "at home" in a female body, J wasn't comfortable anywhere. His spirituality closed down as s/he went from one church to another looking for answers that didn't exist.

There were indications, such as testing positive for color-blindness and being told that "she" had male-pattern baldness, that "she" was not really female. But s/he was trying so hard to be the woman s/he was supposed to be that those were just seen as obstacles. As hard as s/he (and her friends) tried, s/he never managed more than an ambiguous, androgynous look. For the most part s/he avoided doctors (and mirrors). But side effects of the female hormones and lumps in "her" breasts sent J to a new specialist to check on the "hormone problem." That began a series of more tests, including, finally, genetic testing. He remembers vividly the day the doctors sat him down and told him he was intersexed, a genetic male, altered at birth. His initial response was shock and denial, then anger and confusion. He became angry at the doctors who had done this to him, and angry at God.

J's new team of doctors and therapists had little to offer in the way of a road map or role models for him to follow. They advised him to consider all options, including staying identified as a woman. The decision was difficult, considering that he was married with children. But as the female hormones were tapered, he felt a "cloud lifting" and his true self began to emerge. His senses became more acute, and moments of awe at the wonders of nature returned. When testosterone shots were started his body responded like an adolescent's. Shaving for the first time in his mid-thirties was a milestone. His already thinning hair receded, and grew in coarse and curly on his chest. The emotional changes were a roller coaster as he began to find his now deeper male voice, and use it. He went through a distinctive grieving process for all that he had missed out on. There were new losses as well, such as losing his alto singing voice, and many adjustments to make in how people reacted to him. Over time, a profound gratitude emerged as he reclaimed his masculine identity. Picking a new name that included the one his father had chosen for "her" was a healing experience, as he struggled to become a man without sacrificing his gentle compassionate nature. He describes this time as one of psychological and spiritual rebirth.

His family and community relationships, however, were strained by this transformation. He was advised by his medical team to come out slowly and systematically, but with a house full of adolescents in a small town that just wasn't possible. His children each reacted in their own way to his changes. They were more upset by the dissolution of their parents' marriage, and his subsequent "lesbian" relationship. (All but one has since come to appreciate him as neither mother nor father, just a male parent.) Some of their Christian friends were not as charitable about his new journey. Most of his friends were supportive, however, as well as his parents and siblings. He went back to school to establish a new career, and received a standing ovation from his classmates at graduation.

J decided not to pursue sexual "reassignment" surgery (genital reconstruction), given the possibility of losing sexual sensitivity in the process. He began chest reconstruction surgery, to remove some of the benign lumps. Being recognized as his male self was enough. He separated from his spouse and moved to a new community, to spare his kids any embarrassment and to get a fresh start. He became involved in a relationship with a bisexual woman, who was very supportive throughout his transition. Her social support, however, came from the lesbian community, and in the end she wanted to be with a woman, not a straight male. He became active in the FTM (female-to-male) community, and started dating. He found that bisexual women were the most open to becoming intimate, but some were more curious than genuinely interested. He reconciled to the possibility of being alone, and focused on adjusting to his new career in special education. He stayed very involved with his children as they moved into adulthood, helping them with their education and relationships.

The time on his own also renewed his interest in spirituality. Coming back to himself led him back to his relationship with God. The "God in a box" church failed him completely. When he began his transition rumors started about J being a lesbian, and the church community, including the pastor, shut him out cold. To him the Christian faith is about relationship—with people, the earth, and God. A church that did not acknowledge all loving relationships did not work for him. He began exploring other faith traditions, trying Tai Chi and meditation, reading about Buddhism, and simply walking on the beach, to feel the presence of God and the awe of creation once again. He sought a simple, quiet spiritual community, one that was open and inclusive and valued justice, equality of all people, and service. He found that in the Society of Friends; he describes a weekend at a Quaker retreat center as a "homecoming."

Our paths crossed at that intersection of spirituality and diversity. I have experienced myself as bisexual, androgynous, and intensely spiritual for as long as I can remember. Growing up as a tomboy in a rural neighborhood, with older brothers and three boys next door, I had little use for "girl stuff." I was most at home in the woods, climbing trees or building forts in secret places. The girl friends I had were all as horse-crazy as I was, and my imaginary friends were all four-legged, and lived in the "stables" under the pine trees. I have always had special places, in the woods or by a stream, where I could go and sit and experience a sense of peace and wholeness that I can only describe as sacred. I have also always believed in a sexuality that was sacred, and transcended class, race, age, and gender distinctions.

Fortunately, coming of age in the late '60s gave me the opportunity to develop my "sexual theology" in relative safety and freedom. As I moved through college and graduate school I was able to both study and experience alternative lifestyles and alternative spiritual traditions. Buddhism in particular supported the abolition of any distinction between the sacred and the profane, and provided a grounded spiritual practice. I married my first husband in a Buddhist temple, after taking my Refuge vows there. Being openly bisexual, in an open marriage, was not unusual in the Buddhist community. It did not play well in the Midwest, however, where we moved to pursue our academic careers. I retreated into the role of the professor's wife. I taught part-time and focused my energy on our daughter, as my husband became more and more involved in his research. Our spiritual life and our intimacy dwindled. We ended up with separate bedrooms and separate lives. What kept me relatively sane was my connection to nature through gardening and horseback riding.

Somehow body and soul survived, but barely. I left the marriage after cancer claimed my reproductive organs. That ushered in a sexual and spiritual renaissance. Once again I could approach intimate relationships with freedom and openness. My androgynous nature found expression in a variety of ways. It took every ounce of male and female energy to cope with buying and fixing up a house on next to no income, forging new social relationships, and raising an adolescent daughter on my own. I felt myself becoming more alive, whole, and creative than ever before. I have always felt equally at home in ball gowns and blue jeans, but even my style of clothing changed as a more integrated identity emerged. I began to explore new spiritual communities and also started a meditation group based on Buddhist teachings.

When we reflect back on the beginning of our relationship, J likes to thank God for answering his prayers. I thank the computer matchmaker who introduced us. I was casually dating someone an hour away, but still looking for people to do social activities with in my area. J was looking to develop a social life in a new community. The matchmaker had a lengthy questionnaire; we recognized each other as kindred spirits even before we met. I invited him to my meditation group, without any expectations of romance. We had supper afterwards and talked for hours. Several "non-dates" later, we acknowledged the attraction between us. Then J hemmed and hawed and said he had something to tell me before we got more involved. My mind raced through the possibilities—another relationship, a sexually transmitted disease? He took a deep breath and explained that he was intersexed, "kind of like a nonop transsexual," and that most of the women he had been with were lesbian or bisexual. I breathed a sigh of relief—I knew from teaching child development what he was talking about. "I'm attracted to you as a person," I replied, "and I do happen to be bisexual."

That was the beginning of our very special relationship. We have had all the normal adjustments of second marriages and "blended" families. Fortunately the commonality of our beliefs connects us more than the differences divide. Most importantly, we both see our spirituality as part of the fabric of everyday life, including our sexual life, no matter how we express it on any given day. And our spiritual beliefs support us in transcending gender roles and the physical limitations of biological sex.

10

A SPIRITUAL JOURNEY

BARBARA SATIN

AT AGE SIXTY I decided to begin living my life more completely as the woman I had known was hidden within me since age six. For me, that meant leaving a marriage of more than thirty-eight years and devastating the woman who had been my partner for that period. While I have experienced immense joy living primarily as a woman, I have great sadness over the anguish I have caused my wife and the subsequent sorrow my children have felt over seeing their loving parents separated.

This decision also began the spiritual journey of Barbara. At the same time I left my marriage, I also left my church. I realized that there could be no significant role for Barbara in the Catholic church. I decided that rather than begin searching for a new denomination, I would simply live a spiritual life without need for a traditional church home. But only months after I made that decision, I realized that I needed a place and a community of believers with whom to worship and serve my God. I found that home with Spirit of the Lakes United Church of Christ in Minneapolis where I soon became an active member.

Spirit of the Lakes was a predominantly gay, lesbian, bisexual church. When I walked through the front doors on a warm summer Sunday, I presented them with a dilemma. I was the first transgender person to call Spirit of the Lakes my spiritual home. They now had to deal with the "T" in LGBT.

While I have felt welcomed and accepted at Spirit of the Lakes, I know my presence has not been easy for every member. Transgender people are pretty hard to overlook and we come trailing all sorts of misunderstood facts and faulty perceptions. Most church members have worked hard at overcoming disapproval and prejudices. I thank God they were willing to do so.

For the rest of the world, many men—and gay men are no exception—have great difficulty accepting my display of femininity; the clothes, the makeup, and the attitude. Some find it an affront to their masculinity. Others, I like to believe, are just envious or threatened by my femininity. Many women—and lesbian women are no exception—find my fashion style and demeanor hard to deal with. Some view it as a representation of the superficial femininity they have struggled so hard to overcome, while others assume I am mocking their womanhood. None of that is true.

Barbara Satin's goal as a transgendered woman is to help people understand who we as transgender persons really are. My belief is that no one will fully accept us until they have come to know us in our entirety. If I have a calling, a ministry, it is not to my brothers and sisters in our diverse transgender community—they have others who can help them more effectively than I can—but rather my mission is to evangelize the rest of the world around the issue of transgender acceptance.

As part of my spiritual journey, I have had the opportunity to actively participate in the United Church of Christ Coalition for Lesbian, Gay, Bisexual, and Transgender Concerns. Currently, I serve as Moderator of the Coalition, the first transgender person to hold that position. This national group, with local chapters throughout the country, works to keep LGBT issues and needs in front of the denomination and to work on justice issues for all who are lesbian, gay, bisexual, or transgender.

Recently, I was elected to the Board of Directors of the Office of General Ministries and to the Executive Council of the UCC. This opportunity to serve on these leadership groups of the denomination has been an important gift to me because it allows me to offer a transgender presence to the broader Church. Most of my connections with other components of this denomination have been with groups and congregations that are welcoming to the diversity that I represent, even though they may not fully understand it. However, my presence on the Executive Council and the General Ministries Board connects me with members of the denomination who not only don't understand me but, in some cases, may want to find me unacceptable. My challenge is to find ways for them to get to know me and from that knowledge come to better understand who I am and what I represent within this church.

In my view, Church communities of all denominations especially need to experience transgender persons as loving, concerned individuals who worship and serve the same God as the other members of their churches. Neighborhoods need to experience transgender people as involved residents who want the same success and security as the rest of the neighborhood. Society at large needs to experience transgender people as concerned citizens who want peace and justice for everyone—including ourselves.

BREAKTHROUGH

LISA HARTLEY

CULTURALLY INDUCED STRESS DISORDER (CISD) HAPPENS when people gang up on minorities and bully them. There is nothing that we can do about it. If we try to fight back, they'll have us arrested. The majority ⏑ules.

Being one who was a member of the majority and who now is a member of a minority is a powerful experience. I understand that the power culture has can overwhelm me. I feel totally defeated and completely alone. Rage wells up within me and I want to retaliate, to get even. *How dare they treat me this way!* I think. *Who the hell do they think they are, anyhow!* I also know the cultural trap that's set up for me if I act out on my rage. I know I'll be punished, which will only make me angrier, until I simply go crazy, and probably end up in jail. I also know the "traps" that can snag me if I try escaping the reality of being a minority. I could do drugs, or get drunk, or just drop out and do nothing. But I can't do that. I'm wounded but not destroyed. I'll just cry my eyes out and then sleep it off. I'll say a prayer and ask God to rescue me. She always does.

Again and again it happens. Again and again I feel the wounds bleed anew through the scarred tissue of my heart. I become accustomed to my status. They have power. I do not. If I don't challenge them, maybe they will leave me alone.

"Who are *they?*" my counselor asked.

"You know," I replied. "It's everyone. I never know when it's coming or from whom."

"What do you *mean?*" she said.

"I don't know," I replied. "It's just a feeling. I know that because I'm transgendered, everyone will dump on me."

"*Everyone?*" she asked.

"Yea, everyone." I replied. "The whole freakin' world. I just don't care any more." After a tear-filled silence my tears abated. I sat there feeling so empty.

She looked at me tenderly. "I know it's hard, dear," she soothed. "But sometimes I think that you are your own worst enemy. I think that it's easy to believe that the whole world is laughing at you, or scorning you, or . . . just plain rejecting. But, you know, almost anyone can feel that way. We are all a minority of one. We are all alone. We are all different."

"So why do we pick on each other, then?" I asked.

She smiled and said, "If I knew the why of everything, I'd be in such demand that you couldn't afford me!" (We shared a laugh.) "I don't know why, but I know that I can control my own mind, and my own sense of myself. If others don't understand me, or in some way try to put me down, I see it as *their* problem. I can't take on the whole world. I can only do *me*."

We sat, again, in silence. I felt confused. This new way of looking at things seemed okay but— not *totally* okay.

"I see what you are doing," I said, "but isn't there a group thing, a cultural thing that comes into play?"

"A *group* thing?" she asked.

"Yea," I answered, "like culture doesn't like trannies and so it gives everyone the social right to discriminate against us, to wound us, or even to kill us!"

"Hum," she pondered. "Are you saying that the culture is like a unified whole? One that has its own code of conduct? Are you saying that the culture as a group doesn't like trannies, and has agreed to discriminate, wound, and even kill them?"

"Yea," I said, "But when *you* say it, well, it sounds like poop. I mean culture isn't really unified at all, is it?"

She smiled. "I think that you might have hit on something here!" she announced. "Now if culture isn't unified, how is it that they can team up against transgendered people?"

"I know," I replied, "if there was a shared value system or something held in common, like, *you must not change your sex,* then it would seem okay to harm us!"

"Hum," she pondered, "do you think that *everyone* in culture would believe that one mustn't change one's sex?"

"I don't know," I confessed. I felt so frustrated. "I think we'd all be hard pressed to get any universal belief. There are always exceptions."

"*Bingo*!" she replied. "Good for you! Now, who is really giving you poop?"

I sat there in silence once again. As my eyes filled with tears, I whispered, "*Me.*"

She took my hand in hers, looked into my eyes, and smiled warmly. "You've come a long way, today, dear. I am very proud of you. Unfortunately our time is up for today. But there is much for you to ponder until we meet again next week. Okay?"

I dabbed my eyes with a tissue and smiled vulnerably. "I guess you're right," I said. "The world isn't out to get me after all. My challenge is to accept myself; to accept the new me. Not everyone will be cool with it, I know. But maybe I can help them understand. I can explain."

"Hold it, young lady," she said, "You owe no one any explanation. You are you! You are beautiful. You are new. You are real. Educate others if you want. But don't feel that you have to, in order to be accepted. Once you can love who you are, the rest will come. Realize that we all get dumped on. And yes, we also dump on ourselves, too! Some are too fat. Some are too ugly. Some are too butch. Some are too femme. On and on and on it goes. But you, my dear, are beautiful!"

"What about culturally induced stress disorder?" I asked.

"It's interesting," she replied, "But it needs some work. It sets us up to believe that everyone is on the same page, which obviously we are not. But it has potential. Next week, same time?"

"Yes," I said. "I've got some thinking to do and some revisions to make."

As I drove home I thought, "Oh my God. I've written about CISD and talked about it until I was blue in the face. What now?" I felt so embarrassed. Once at home sitting there with my writings, I decided to read the stuff over. I was almost drawn into the gist of it again. Fortunately, I didn't allow myself to be. It seemed my head was clearing. Yes, there was an error in sex assignment at birth. Yes, no one knew it was an error. Yes, I was socialized in the gender role that matched my assigned sex identity at birth. But there was no ill intended. These were good people who were happy to bring me into this world.

Yes, I became aware of being different. Yes, I longed to be a girl, but couldn't explain why. Yes, it was a struggle to behave in ways that the world outside me wanted me to be. And, yes, I found a way to satisfy my needs by fantasizing about *being* a girl.

Yes, I cried in private, when my prayers were not answered by the "miracle." And, yes, I felt unsure of myself and felt that I was not as good as everyone else.

Yes, I joined the Marines to beat this yearning for womanhood out of me and help me learn how to be a man. And, yes, I went to college and got a Masters degree. Yes, I married and had two lovely children, a boy and a girl. I became a Roman Catholic and joined all the committees, was a Eucharistic Minister, and taught CCD (Confraternity of Christian Doctrine), the way all "new" Catholics do.

And, no, it didn't work: the Marines, the degree, the marriage and the kids, the church, or anything else. It wasn't meant to work.
But yes, there was a stronger urging to be me—a relentless urging so familiar to me. It was the urging to be a woman: to be me.

It cost me. It cost my marriage to a good woman; the love of two lovely kids; the loss of my own brother; the loss of respect at work and in my own profession that I'd always been and continue to be so proud to serve; and the loss of understanding from the Church.

But you know what? Now, I *am* me. I actually did it. Oh, there were those who were afraid for me. Those who said I was crazy, delusional, and on and on. But, hey, guess what! I am me. At last I am at peace within my previously tortured soul—a peace that I had only dreamed of before. I am real. I am! Yeah, baby!

And you know what else? If the "culture" didn't allow me to transition from male to female, I wouldn't have been able to find a doctor who cared for my physical and hormonal needs. I wouldn't have found an accepting therapist, who loved me for *me*. I wouldn't have found a colleague, who was also my boss, to support me as I transitioned on my job. I wouldn't have found the tenderness of so many that I ignored, while on my silly tirade against a few stupid people I misnamed "the culture." I wouldn't have found so many new friends at the support groups and online. I wouldn't have found anyone who would write letters in support of me to change my name, change my driver's license, and change my birth records. And I wouldn't have found a surgeon who would make me physically complete for the first time in my entire life.

And you know what else? If it wasn't for the dedicated scientists here and throughout the world, I would still be wondering how I got this way.

There are no laws that say, "transgendered people are not allowed here." No one is going to arrest me for being who I am, thanks to those who came before me—they forged the pathway. There are no clubs whose purpose is to rid the earth of transgendered persons.

Yet I am not totally freaking out here. I know there are challenges. There always will be. We can be our own worst enemy or we can enjoy who we are, whatever that may be. There will always be our detractors, but you know what? There are more people who support us today than ever before! And you know what else? The future couldn't be brighter.

I developed the concept "culturally induced stress disorder" (CISD). So I can revise it too. We do struggle. We do need support. But it is not the tome, the dirge that I'd constructed. I was wrong. In fact, I can't stand it any more. I don't need to be dragging everybody down. I need to respect who I am! The stages of the struggle are there for all of us in our own journey, but instead of stages of pain and disorder, these are stages of a healthy courageous search for our own human truth, our own victory!

We need to work *together*: TVs (transvestites), TSs (transsexuals), MTFs (male-to-females), FTMs (female-to-males), androgynes, and everyone else in our community. We need to continue the momentum of acceptance that is beginning to really happen! We can and will stand proudly in our freedom to be —to be free, to be ourselves, and to make this world a better place because we are here.

THE CHALLENGE AND THE GIFT

"Now I lay me down to sleep, I pray the Lord my soul to keep. If I should die before I wake, I pray the Lord my soul to take. Amen."

How many times I prayed that prayer! Then, after being tucked in for the night, and making sure that I was alone, I whispered another prayer. "God. Are you still there? I hope so. I've been trying hard to be good. I know you do miracles. Please God, do a miracle for me. During the night when I'm asleep, please come and make me a girl. I'll do anything you want, but please make me a girl. Amen."

I always awoke to find that God didn't make me a girl—at least by doing a miracle in *that* way. After many years and many tears, I learned that God had performed that miracle on me before I was born. My brain was female. But my genitals were male. Everyone said that I was a boy. But God and I knew better. She had given me a challenge. She had also given me the courage to face the many challenges that were to come. Once I found the courage to face and accept the truth of my true sex identity that is expressed in my brain, my journey became clear.

And now the challenges are from culture. I must share my knowledge and my understanding of transgender, with the hope that you will understand the truth, and then respond with compassion to help transgendered people. The emotional and physical wounding of transgendered people must stop.

Many times in my journey I fell into despair; and many times I feel so all alone. Then, I pray for help and God comes to rescue me. I am thankful that God is never too far away. God strengthens me so that I can carry on and share my gift with you. God's gift to me is my gift to you. My difference is a reality to celebrate. Indeed, *all* human differences are gifts to celebrate and share with one another. I hope that you will agree. I hope that you will share your gift with me too. I love you.

12

THE PHOENIX WILL FLY

Nickolas J. McDaniel

What is the bigger crime? To alter my existence with suicide or my body in the pursuit of contentment? Both are sins against God and humanity, they tell me.

If both are wrong, which is the bigger evil? Which outweighs the other? What if those are the only choices—suicide or transsexualism? I guess the answer lies in what each person believes. If changing my body is a sin, why did God instill within me the instinct to survive? For me, masculinizing hormones and sexual reassignment surgery (SRS) was the only option if I did not want to die.

After seeing the miserable creature I was—seething with sadness and unable to function—and the strides I have made in my life over the past two years while post-op and on testosterone, is there any question of the validity of hormones and SRS in my case? There are so many people questioning gender and sexuality, each with his/her own unique twist. Many are having dire problems as bad as I had . . . some much, much worse. Could they rise up from the fire to be reborn just as I have done?

In order to survive, some transsexuals have sold their bodies to accumulate funds for sex reassignment surgery and therapy. Are they sinners because they sold bodies they never owned in order to facilitate a change to become productive members of society or in the pursuit of happiness?

Treatment for transsexualism is cost effective. Even though extremely expensive, it is significantly less than a lifetime of psychotropic drugs, hospitalizations, and emergency services with no significant employment or benefit to society. With the help of SRS and testosterone, I am beginning to merge with society, returning to college with the desire not only to support myself but to devote my life to the community that carried me for so long.

For me, the cleansing of my birth gender has made all the difference. Just as the phoenix emerges from the flames to be reborn, transsexuals are reborn from adversity. To fly or burn is up to each person. Fasten your seatbelts! If you are flying with me, it'll be a hell of a long ride! Count on it!

As a female to male (FTM) post-op transsexual, I feel thwarted by religions that recognize me as a sinner. God is perfect, they preach, so the altering of my body through human means is a sin. God would not make a mistake! Brought up in the Southern Baptist church, I always heard the "fire and brimstone" our preacher spouted like a volcano spewing molten lava. It always struck me as hateful and elitist. It was a garment many sizes too small for the ideology within my heart. I got bruised and burned, so therefore I revolted.

As a victim of incest and mental manipulation, I considered that if God makes no mistakes, then the hell I endured at home I must deserve. I wondered why my own heart said I was a boy but my female body denied it. I began to hate God and myself. I fled into the arms of self-mutilation and suicide. My main goal in life was to end it.

I spent ten years in and out of caring medical facilities. I was a regular patient who believed suicide was my only friend. I had been betrayed by my body. I had been betrayed by God.

I gave myself until I was thirty years old—set the bar, so to speak to see if this dark depression I was in would lift. If not, I was going to check out. Having been a disciple of suicide, I had studied death closely. I was ready.

Just before my twenty-ninth birthday, things in me began to change so that the possibility of changing my body to become congruent with my mind through testosterone and surgery became a reality. Those spiritual burns began to heal.

With each accomplishment—winning funding for top surgery from MediCal and dropping one hundred pounds so I could begin hormones—bits of scab flecked from the burns upon my heart. New pink flesh peeked through warily and I began to see a higher being in the beautiful wonder of flora and fauna. I became fascinated with all that was alive.

My personal belief is that God is not the idealized white male. Jesus may not have brown hair and blue eyes that I see in this idealized European American culture. He or she may not hate me. He or she is not perfect.

I love living. I love my body, though it is still not perfect. I love whatever entity created all about me. And it may sound egotistical, but I love myself and even those that hate me for being me.

13

A PLACE AT THE TABLE [1]

STEPHANIE RODRIGUEZ

ABOUT THE TIME I feel I have no lessons left to learn in my Christian life, God will bring out one more. I would like to share something I found out recently about myself and prejudice. A few of you have heard this anecdote, so bear with me.

Prejudice, bigotry, bias—they are all such ugly words and uglier still when their effects have been leveled at you. As members of Affirmation! (a United Methodist LGBT affinity group), we all share some level of concern about our place in American society and particularly our place within the United Methodist Church. We long for those places to be better, to have parity. Within the teachings of Christ we hear love and acceptance, but within the organization of the church we have a Book of Discipline that spells out our place in rather painful terms.

Experiencing so much open, systematic, vocal rejection by what should be the very instrument of Christian love has really been difficult for me. Over the years I evolved from closeted and ultraconservative to essentially open and liberal. I definitely understood the need for acceptance, tolerance, love thy neighbor, and so on.

Only I didn't. You see, my "neighbor" was defined as anyone who was already a lot like me, or who thoughtfully kept their distance and did not offend or challenge. What an utterly shameful position for a Christian to take. The thing is, that position was so long-term, so much a background to my day, that I was not even aware of it.

When national Affirmation! requested a forum for transsexuals, I openly questioned what this had to do with us. I felt it unnecessary and offensive. Well, apparently God did not, because within a few weeks circumstances pushed me grudgingly into conversation with a well-known local transsexual. The conversation was innocuous and the content irrelevant, but the epiphany that occurred for me immediately altered my life.

I was suddenly so aware of, and ashamed of, my selfishness—and astonished that these feelings had smoldered long past the point where I considered myself insightful and devout. Since then I have made it my daily practice to be alert for other times that I may reject or disenfranchise some person or group.

I relate this story to you because I believe it so important for us . . . to be sure that our focus includes *making* a place at the table, not just *gaining* one. When our thoughts, our conversations, or our humor are self-deprecating or exhibit prejudice or bigotry toward others, we are debilitating our spiritual selves and thwarting our real desire—to have a full relationship with our God.

I frequently ask myself, "Have I been forgiving today? Have I been compassionate?" To these questions I now add, "Whom have I sent away?"

NOTES

1. From *Transgender Pocket,* copyright © 2000, the UCC Coalition for Lesbian, Gay, Bisexual, and Transgender Concerns. Used by permission.

14

MY LIFE STORY

JACOB NASH

I WAS BORN IN A SMALL TOWN in Massachusetts on November 17, 1964. Right from the start God had big plans for me! I was brought up in a Baptist home with a Catholic dad, which made for interesting conversations at times. My faith has always been important to me, going as far back as I can remember.

I remember when I was thirteen and getting ready to be baptized. It was March 18, 1977. In preparing for this big day the class had to meet with the minister of our church to see if we were ready. I knew this was a big step and I had already decided years earlier that I wanted to become a youth pastor. I remember our pastor asking me if I knew what being baptized was all about. I remember wondering if all the other kids knew how important this step was and that it could change your life. God was involved in my life; nothing could change that!

As the years went on I graduated from high school and went on to college. My goal of becoming a youth pastor stayed the same. Yet as I worked towards that goal, my enthusiasm dwindled and I became discouraged with the pettiness of church doctrines. It seemed, from my friendships with other youth pastors, that when you were involved with one particular church, you had to slavishly follow a prescribed set of narrow beliefs.

College was very hard for me as my life struggles took over. Depression set in. The dislike I had for myself was overwhelming! My junior year in college was the first time I tried to commit suicide. For me, suicide was to get away from my problems and be at home with God. That was my goal, but God had other plans for me!

Looking back over my younger years I noticed how very much alone and secluded I was. I hated myself and my body, but I didn't know why. Why was I so uncomfortable when it came to physical interaction with people of the opposite sex (at that time it was men)? I dated boys—that's what I was supposed to do. But I hated kissing them. I liked hanging with them, but when the boys wanted more, it threw me into a tail spin. What was wrong with me? Life seemed to get more and more complicated.

I tried to commit suicide. I could have kicked myself when I woke up in the hospital after my attempt. Everyone at the college knew about it, so the rumors where flying! I couldn't handle all the stares and gossip so I decided to transfer. I went to a bigger college where I could get lost. My previous school only had a total of one hundred students or so; my new one had ten times that many. It was easier for me to get lost. But my faith stayed strong.

"God, how am I going to make it? I know I need to stay close to you but, boy, am I having a tough time of things! My grades are poor. I'm fighting with my folks because my grades are poor. I hate my body. Boys want to get more physical with me than I want . . . *help*!"

College graduation came and went in 1988; now what was I going to do with my life? I had the degree that I always wanted but I didn't know where or how I wanted to use it. I worked at a camp for a year as a cook and then started working in a residential home for emotionally disturbed adolescents. I loved my job. I hunted for a church family I could become part of that could use the gifts that God had given me. Not only did I have a desire to work with youth, I also played guitar and sang. By 1990 I found a church and things started to look up for me. Then I was diagnosed with ulcerative colitis. That hit me hard and fast. I could no longer work a regular job. I could not be as active in my church as I would have liked to be. "Okay, God, what now"? As all this was hitting me I fell in love with a woman! How could this happen? I am not a lesbian, but I loved this relationship that was growing. As the relationship progressed I realized that the dynamics between us were getting more complex. I liked being with a woman but it didn't feel quite right either. "God, where is this all going"? "Oh God, my help in ages past, my hope for years to come." The lyrics to that hymn rang clear. While all this stuff was coming to the forefront of my life, my security was in Jesus. My life was now forever changed but I went back to what I was told is normal—the guy/girl relationship.

It was 1996 and I got married to a man. Even though my heart was not in it, I convinced myself that things would be better after I got married and the "feelings" that I felt towards men would change! How come I still felt this way? How come when my husband touched me it made me feel sick inside? How come when we made love I couldn't wait till it was over?

During this time in my life it seemed like everything was going the way it was supposed to go. I was married. I was very active in my church. I had a good job working at a bank. I had a successful Christian band that was playing every other weekend. I was recording my first professional tape and my relationship with God was growing in leaps and bounds.

What happened? It all started to fall apart in December of 1996. I could not live a lie any more! I separated from my husband. Because of this I lost the band, my church, some friends—but I never lost my faith. My divorce became final in May 1998. As I sat watching TV one day, I was changing the channels and caught a show on the Discovery channel about a woman who had a sex change operation and was now a man.

As I sat watching this it was like a light bulb went on in my head, "That's it, that's what is wrong with me!" I ran and told my girlfriend (after I separated from my husband I became involved with another woman). From then on my whole outlook on life was different. It was as if my life started over. I really prayed about what it meant to be transgendered. I prayed constantly for God to help me to make the right decision. I searched the Bible to see what, if anything, it had to say about changing your sex. I just prayed for God's guidance. Would this be okay in God's eyes? I so much wanted to do what was right by God. I wanted God to bless me and my life.

I remember the first time I went to talk with the specialists at the Gender Clinic in Connecticut. They were wonderful and very professional. I would soon be on my way to starting hormones and living the "real life test." Four and a half years and many surgeries later my life is becoming complete. I finally can look at myself and like who I am! I have a wonderful woman in my life named Erin who supports me and loves me for who I am and the man I am becoming. Hopefully one day we will be legally married. I no longer struggle with the physical aspects of a relationship since I have become my true gender!

My love for God grows every day! Without God I would not be the man I am today. God has truly been beside me, guiding me through this journey. God has provided everything I have needed in my life, and more. I am still searching for a church that will accept the whole me and not judge me because I am transgender. I have so much to give and desire to use it to glorify God, who has touched my life in such a profound way. I would not have been able to make it through all the changes in my life if I had not had Jesus to look to for help and guidance. Every step of the way he has shown himself faithful.

15

A FUNERAL FOR MY "HUSBAND"

ELLA MATHESON WITH LAUREN HAYWOOD

YOU MIGHT THINK IT'S CRAZY when I tell you that I held a funeral for my spouse while he was still "alive." A funeral normally signifies closure—the death of a whole person. In the transgender community, some spouses might understand this need for closure. Their transgender partners, on the other hand, might ask "Why get upset? After all, it's the same person." Before my husband Scott's transition I would have said "If it is the same person, then why the need to transition in the first place?" I found myself crying off and on for months at losing my beloved Scott to his new persona as Shelly.

In 1981 I fell in love with, and later married, a gorgeous, six-foot-two, handsome, muscular, gentle giant with a hairy chest and back. Given Scott's size and body type there was no way I could have ever imagined him as a woman. Scott was my even-tempered, keenly intelligent Prince Charming. I'd never met anyone like him, the kind of man who put me at ease whenever he was near. The more hours we spent together, the closer we got. As a heterosexual couple, we'd enjoyed the insular bubble of privacy that seemed to surround us. People stepped aside, waiters were less intrusive, and, in general, people were more respectful of our privacy when they found us engaged in conversation—a level of privacy not allotted to us as two females.

At the beginning of Scott's transition, we were living in Europe. None of our friends or colleagues there knew anything about Scott's situation. Our European support system was large, consisting mostly of friends from the conservative, evangelical Christian community. Within that world, we were often considered the epitome of what the perfect happily married couple should be. The problem was that this type of community tolerates little diversity, especially when it concerns questions of gender. For the first several years of our marriage, I had felt secure and relaxed in the knowledge that my "man" was in charge. I sincerely believed that Scott had my best interest at heart. Little did I know just how much my husband was suffering in order to maintain his masculine facade.

As an evangelical Christian, I believed that changing my husband's body, changing his sex, was a sin. I was horrified at the prospect of Scott's male body morphing into a feminine one. I also worried constantly about what other people would think. I was terrified that others would no longer see us as good Christians. But most of all, I worried that this transition would end our relationship. Scott and I were soul mates. Therefore, I was desperate to keep our relationship exactly the way it had always been—very close, secure, and stable. We had married relatively young, both in our twenties. I was extremely insecure and very naive—naive enough to think that my husband's "problem," a problem he'd told me about before we were married, would somehow just go away.

Then around 1992, Scott began to fall apart emotionally. He'd been cross-dressing on rare occasions for the first nine years of our marriage—a situation that made us both feel uncomfortable. As a good Christian, I feared Scott would destroy his life wallowing in a sinful vice if he continued with his obsession. What I couldn't see then was how the weight of acting out his false identity as a male was taking its toll on his emotions. Later that year the pressure became too much for Scott, and we decided to fly to London to find an English-speaking gender counselor. It was also at that point that we hooked up with the transgender network and began attending conferences.

At one of those conferences, I met Barbara, the wife of another transgender person, a fiery petite woman with a passion for oil painting. Barbara's passion appealed to me, as my heart's desire had always been to be a successful artist. I'd been working as a computer specialist, having moved away from my training in visual arts. Classical painting had fascinated me since about the age of twelve, though it hadn't been part of my arts education. I'd actually spent some time hunting in Europe for a painting teacher, but to no avail.

Barbara and I became fast friends. The first time we visited Barbara and her husband, Thomas, in New England, I fell in love with the elegant beauty and craft of classical oil painting. Eventually, I gave up my work with computers to begin a long-distance apprenticeship with Barbara's painting teacher. As my painting skills improved, so did my self-esteem. It seemed ironic that this profound and exciting career change had come through a transgender connection, a community that, at the time, I considered very suspect.

I still had a very hard time accepting the fact that my husband was really a woman. Why couldn't Scott stay a man if he loved me? I fought each stage of his transition as though I was fighting for my life. With each new phase came overwhelming waves of fear. The Shelly side of Scott began to emerge after several years of cross-dressing. Cross-dressing led into three years of electrolysis.

Still terrified that the inevitable would come to pass, I prayed that God would direct Scott to remain a man for me. Then at some point, I began to realize that all Scott's stress came down to the issue of him trying to be the "man" he knew I wanted him to be. Knowing that he couldn't carry on this way much longer, he was also afraid of how his change would affect me.

In 1988, after many years of debating whether or not to move forward, we finally agreed that Scott should go ahead with hormone injections. This first dose, I was told, would only be a minuscule amount—just enough to calm Scott's raging frustration, hardly enough to effect our sex life. As the dosages increased, small breasts developed, and our sex life evaporated—there was no going back. Although each phase seemed to be followed by some manner of relief, it never lasted long. Scott was happy on estrogen; the problem was that he still had to act like a man and bottle up who he really was. At that point, he became depressed, thinking that he would have to live in limbo for the rest of his life. My husband's deepest desire was to eliminate the false image of his male self—the very same image that I found so real, so solid.

Due to our unusual situation, we were losing, and letting go of, our old support system from the church. At that same time, we were also making new friends like Barbara and Thomas who were instrumental in helping us change our lives. After connecting with the transgender community we met Joe, another transsexual who'd not yet transitioned. Joe was, and still is, one of most spiritual people I've ever met. He'd been a Pentecostal minister and his spiritual example, more than anything else, helped me realize that it would be possible to be simultaneously transgender and spiritually mature. Joe reassured me that God's answers to our prayers aren't as direct as we might want them to be. I had always put my faith in Jesus to help me through life, everything from finding a parking space to major life changes, like marriage and moving to Europe. Now more than ever, I had to lean on God to help me through the double crisis that was about to unfold in our lives.

Believing that there were no shortcuts through the fire, I leaned on God, trusting in the ultimate plan for my life. As my own sense of self-confidence rose, I began to exhibit a maturity that allowed me, for the first time, to make my own decisions. Therefore, worrying about what the neighbors would think lost its potency in shaping my decisions.

Then came the day when hormones and electrolysis weren't enough, and our fireside conversations began. Scott would come home from work and build a roaring fire. The two of us talked endlessly about our options as the flames slowly warmed our bodies. Wrapped in blankets, we stared into the fire discussing the pros and cons of our decisions until finally we came to the conclusion that it was best for Scott to move forward and fully transition.

Around this same time, I was diagnosed with breast cancer. Scott and I were both devastated by this news. I was already forty pounds overweight when the breast cancer hit. I gained another ten during my chemotherapy due to a lack of activity. With all this extra weight, I felt like a beached whale. My body was a pasty and sickly color from the chemotherapy, yet Scott saw me as beautiful—he still loved me. With all that my body had gone through Scott still saw me as his precious wife. As this realization sunk in, a tinge of shame crept over me. Why couldn't I accept the changes that were going on in Scott's body? After all, this was my soul mate, Scott, who was only trying to be at peace with himself.

Why couldn't I accept him the way he felt he really was? Real love after all, I told myself, doesn't require superficial beauty. It goes much deeper. One needs to look into the very soul of another to see his or her inner beauty. I loved Scott, and if he could see past the image of my "beached whale" body, then I could see past the superficial feminine characteristics that he was developing.

Six months after I finished chemotherapy, Scott's transition to Shelly was in full force and we moved back to the United States to start a new life as two women. En route, we visited my friend Barbara. I was still very weak, dispirited, and sickly from the chemotherapy. I was losing my husband and my identity as a married woman. My friends were evaporating, and I was closing myself off from the few I had left. It felt like death, yet I still hadn't gone through an official funeral. When I told Shelly I wanted to have a burial for her male persona she was horrified. She felt some part of me had to be rejecting her. Yet I was experiencing a death—a very real loss. I felt sad and dreadful at the same time. Where were the friends that should have been rallying around me? It wasn't their fault—most of them didn't even know. It had to be this way.

Jokingly, I suggested to my friend, Barbara, that I needed a funeral. Barbara took it seriously. She thought it was a good idea. Shelly didn't agree. But by that time, I'd gotten a germ of independence. I decided I really needed this funeral—a ritual, a formal acknowledgment of the loss I was experiencing. At the same time, Barbara confessed to me that she was having a terrible time dealing with the loss of her very active sex life with Thomas. At first Barbara wanted to hire a member of the clergy to conduct the funeral. I tried to imagine talking to a minister in robes—explaining why we wanted to have a dual funeral for a lost sex life and the death of an image. Finally, I let Barbara know that for me, the important aspects of a funeral were the eulogy, the acknowledgment of what was lost, singing, and covered dishes—lots of covered dishes to sustain us during our grieving—not the minister.

We planned a dawn funeral for just the two of us—no one else would have understood. Soon excitement began to grip us. This was going to be a real event. We found boxes for our symbols of loss. I washed and carefully ironed Scott's favorite pair of faded jeans and a sports shirt. Barbara took a cucumber as a symbol of her loss. She placed the cucumber in a box with X-rated pictures of couples having sex that she'd downloaded from the Internet. We wrapped our symbols in blue shiny paper, picked out rocks from her driveway to use as grave stones—a smooth stone for me, an incredibly phallic one for Barbara. Then we gathered water and posthole diggers, a shovel, and two lawn chairs for our ritual. Barbara stayed up most of the night copying hymns off the Internet.

We woke before dawn and carried our things out to a designated spot in her backyard, a beautiful place overlooking the pond with a thick mist steaming up over its surface. When the first cracks of blue light filtered over the horizon we built a big bonfire and stated our intentions into the dawn mist. Then we threw our boxes into the fire and watched as they burned down to ash. Next, we wrote down all the things we missed about not having husbands on heart-shaped pieces of paper and dropped them into the roaring flames. Barbara and I talked for awhile; we also sang a few hymns and cried. Above us we saw the sky fill with Canada geese in V formation as they headed south for the winter. Then we sang, "Morning Has Broken" to the yellow beams of light cracking over the edge of the rolling fields just ahead of us.

Finally, through this small ritual, Barbara and I were able to formally acknowledge what we had lost. We sobbed and laughed and burned pictures of Scott and Thomas in little heart-shaped frames with gold borders. After an hour or so, the bonfire burned down and we shoveled dirt over the pit. By that time, the mist had burned off the pond and the day was starting to stir. With the funeral completed, it was time to eat. After breakfast at a nearby diner we went to a restaurant and ordered fifty dollars worth of food for the "covered dish" part of our ritual.

Barbara and I hadn't told anyone about our early morning funeral. I was determined to keep it a secret. But when Shelly returned that evening, I felt so uplifted that I rushed to the driveway and told her everything. To my surprise, Shelly joined in the fun. We were laughing about the day's events when Thomas walked up and innocently asked if we knew where the cucumber was that he'd left in the refrigerator. He'd wanted to include it in our salad for that night's dinner. I looked over at Shelly, and for the first time ever, I saw a new twinkle in my beloved's eye. A huge smile broke across Shelly's face, and we both doubled over in laughter.

16

MY SPIRITUAL JOURNEY

JANICE JOSEPHINE CARNEY

MY ANCESTRAL ROOTS LIE in the French and Irish Christian culture. I was raised by Catholic parents who never entered a church, except on Easter, Christmas, or when seeking much needed substance assistance from the church. I was raised on shame and guilt about my most inner feelings and desires. Sex was a taboo subject; even as I went through most of my years of puberty being sexually molested, it remained a dark secret.

From early on in my life I had a sense that all this boy stuff just was not for me. As soon as I expressed this, it was *strongly* impressed on me that I was a boy, and boys dress and act in one way and girls dress and act in another way. So what does this have to do with my spirituality? *A lot!*

By the time I was old enough to break away from my childhood molester and realize in my very being that I was a woman stuck with male body parts, my intellect and my spirit were broken. The church, the schools, my parents had built into me a core of shame and guilt. I went into the army after high school with a goal of dying in Vietnam and making my family proud of me. A Higher Power had other plans for me. I returned from my three years in the army an agnostic.

Through the middle '70s I was a gender outlaw, living as a trannie sex worker, my soul swelling with guilt and shame, my intellect swept away by alcohol and drugs. In a way, my Catholic guilt and shame saved my life. I purged myself of the woman I was, I got married, I got a series of real jobs. For over twenty years I was a functioning alcoholic. I was a functioning Episcopalian. By 1991, my Higher Power had blessed me with a year of sobriety. At that time I was the junior warden of my church in New Hampshire, sitting as a voting member of the church's vestry. The hot issue in the parish was inviting a gay unordained minister from Massachusetts into our church. This would open the door for him to become an ordained minister. I went through an internal struggle during these meetings, which climaxed with my shouting match with the senior warden of our church. The God of his belief would not allow a gay minister in his church. The God of his belief would forgive a man for killing another man but would not forgive a man for making love to a fellow man. In short, I came out all over the place. The last two years of Alcoholics Anonymous (AA) had freed me of my demons. We voted to accept that man as our new deacon.

Not long after this my charade as a man came to an end. The only way I could stay sober and drug free was to follow my path as a woman. This same church that opened its heart to a gay minister could not extend its embrace for a transsexual. I found intellectual fulfillment in studying the spiritual history of transgender people—the Navajos' *nadle*, the Cheyennes' *he mann eh,* the Lakotas' *Winktes,* the great Joan of Arc burned at the stake. I discovered a vast past of honor placed on transgendered souls. In my mind I came to realize that I was blessed, not cursed with my female/male spirit.

This is how I found myself here in the Unitarian Universalist (UU) Church. A year after leaving my former church, my spirit still was lacking the human contact that a Sunday morning gathering brings. I had been involved with Boston's Arlington Street Church for years as a safe haven from my gender struggle, but needed to find a church closer to home. So I went to the UU church in Manchester, New Hampshire. I found the biggest embrace that I had ever felt in my life. I found the warm loving support that saw me through the last stages of my transition. I received funding for my expenses to Colorado for my surgery by performing my play to a packed church hall. I was overwhelmed with get-well cards while in the hospital. During my slow painful recovery, church members brought me cooked meals and ran errands for me. I have found the spiritual food that my soul craves here in the accepting arms of the Unitarian Universalist Church. Blessed be.

17

JOANNA LOUISE

Oh, you, my sisters and brothers—
you are the beautiful promise of wholeness
for me . . .
and for my brothers and my sisters everywhere
who are fractured by this difference.
Like the Monarch is the symbol,
the symbol of our struggle . . .
of our death . . .
of our entombment . . .
of our captivity . . .
of our resurrection, too . . .
. . . our wholeness . . .
. . . our meaningfulness . . .
of our newfound beauty, too.

Your life shows
the promise of God fulfilled,
the promise . . .
"See I make all things new!"

Oh, take hope, my fractured fellow creatures,
though the struggle is long,
though the tomb is frightening,
though the captivity is painful,
though the adjustments at first are awkward.

When you soar as with the Monarch, friends . . .
know your wholeness sure,
know your meaning true,
take your fullness and then
. . . say, "I'm Me!"

You are at long last the beautiful You . . .
Child of the living God in full bloom . . .
and God's truth has set you free . . .
. . . to be You!
. . . All else will pass away.
You are!
Rejoice!
Praise God!
and doctors, too!

Rise with the Monarch . . .
try your wings . . .
and with the angels converse . . .
and the flowers, too!

Be in the world with your beauty,
and with your beauty . . .
and your love . . .
help God make our whole world new,
as you live thanksgiving . . .
for being made whole . . .

beautiful . . .
meaningful . . .
. . . loving!
So be beautiful,
be meaningful,
be loving,
to all mortal kind!

Whenever you see the Monarch fly . . .
say, "Hello, brother, sister . . .
Thank you for showing the way . . .
so that I may, like you . . .
be the real Me!"

18

MY STORY

S H E R Y L   S T E W A R T

I AM FULLY FEMALE-IDENTIFIED and have been this way since I can remember thinking at all. Of course, I was aware that my body did not agree with my attitude and others' expectations. I felt alone and suspected I was crazy because of the sheer number of people who did not accept me the way I felt. Especially significant was the opinion of the people I loved. So I compromised for many years, orbiting like an airplane in a holding pattern between pretending at a gender I didn't feel I fit in, but which my body seemed superficially suited for (male) and between living, as often as I could for as long as I could, like any other girl. After my parents had both died, I felt there was no longer a compelling enough reason to keep up an increasingly oppressive lie, and I opted for an honesty many still refuse to accept.

I was truly concerned that someone might actually have problems in their faith relationship with God if they saw their pastoral leader pursue a gender reassignment. I, therefore, left the active parish ministry I had been engaged in for fourteen years at the same time I left the onerous and intermittent illusion of masculinity. Well aware that I would be unlikely to find placement after SRS (sexual reassignment surgery), I worked my way up from HHHA (Homemaker Home Health Aide) to RN over the course of about four to five years—and I did all of this as a woman. Ironically, because I was moving from the clergy to health care, I did not experience the economic crunch many transgender women do when they leave male-dominated professions. As a nurse, I earn about two and a half times my highest previous annual salary, and I can do it being honest about myself.

A transsexual is in a bit of a "catch-22" situation regarding honesty. Some people feel that insisting you are one gender while your body has the wrong chromosome is a lie. However, although I know I am a trans-sexual, I don't feel like some kind of in-between or third sex. I feel like I am a woman who was always a woman, as opposed to someone who "be-came" female. I just happen to be a woman who has the singularly dis-comforting knowledge of what it means to try to pass oneself off (fairly effectively) as a male because that is what is expected of her.

I've had MTF (male-to-female) transgender friends who are far prettier than I—they could "pass" as genetic females in bikinis, for heaven's sake—but they still get hung up on appearance. I call it the "Barbie factor." I think we, like most women, get too hung up on anything that isn't drop-dead gor-geous about ourselves. The result is lack of confidence, and confidence is 75 percent (or more) of what helps you pass as your internal gender.

If there is dissonance between the body and the soul, I like to re-member that the body was shaped out of earth by God, but that the spirit is actually God's living breath breathed into the husk. I firmly believe it is more honest to be true to the living breath of God that moves within me than it is to "obey the clay."

The question is sometimes asked: "If you like guys, why aren't you gay?" The question wrongly assumes I am male. So, right off, we aren't on the same wavelength. My body was male—once. Even then, I couldn't consider myself male. I was just too female-identified, even when I vainly tried to please everyone by schooling and, later, working as a male. At last, I decided I couldn't minister being so essentially dishonest as to hide my gender, and I actively entered therapy, got hormones, and began to live as a woman. To be fair to the parish, I left active ministry before the "real life test," the time I began living female all the time.

Following SRS, I wanted continued contact with the few living rela-tives who hadn't utterly disowned me. I had developed a second career, nursing, which I hoped would develop into a nursing ministry. In fact, I could pulpit supply, be active in my local association, and volunteer as a chaplain. However, active parish ministry has not been an option yet. I am very open about my TG journey in my profile; this is doubtless the reason for the profound silence in ministerial invitations beyond an initial letter of inquiry. I am happy with my involvement in ministry, but if I'd counted on continuing to earn my living this way, I'd be homeless.

I also chose to be honest in personal relationships. Sooner or later, a guy was going to find out I had the wrong set of chromosomes. Doug, Bill, and a couple other guys I dated took this as a plus, figuring they'd never have to deal with an unwanted pregnancy—most other men ran away. Gay guys, at least, knew I was a woman all along and, rightly, sought out men who liked men and who really wanted to stay men during the relationship.

Ultimately, the guy I fell in love with was a pre-op FTM transsexual (go figure)! He understands where I am coming from and started dating me shortly after my SRS. So, we had no "body change" conflicts to deal with. After a year of courting, we had a "holy union," which we felt united us in the sight of God. A surprising diversity of clergy and laity attended this ceremony, hosted at the time by some friends from the UFMCC (Universal Fellowship of Metropolitan Community Churches). By the way, I never sought ministry there because my faith home remains United Church of Christ/Disciples of Christ.

As for my husband's physical and social changes, he just moves more into my comfort zone as he goes along! I fell into my present relationship with a best friend! In 2002, we are just past the tenth year from our holy union and it looks to be well on the way to forever. This is with a man who shares my faith, certainly understands my TG journey, accepts me fully as a woman, and could handle the transition of my surgery.

There exists a debate over when an MTF should consider herself a woman. Doubtless, this issue also arises with my FTM brothers. My own approach is to accept someone as the gender of their spirit regardless of their progress (if any, if ever) toward SRS. If someone is bigendered, I tend to accept them as the gender of their presentation in the "present" moment. If their gender changes five times a day, I accept them five different ways that day, altering as appropriately as I am able during the interaction. Some post-op women will only accept a sister into their invisible sorority when she is post-op. I respect their opinion, but that is too limiting for me to embrace. "Do not judge, or you too will be judged. For . . . with the measure you use, it will be measured to you" (Matt. 7:1–2 NIV). A cross-dresser who has no intention of ever having surgery, for example, is expressing a feminine side of his/her spirit during the moment he/she actively dresses. For those moments, cross-dressers are my sisters. Granted, they may decide to become my brothers at any given time and that can be disconcerting or disorienting, but that does not change the fact that there is a girlfriend in there somewhere. Many of the folk who limit TG activity to clothing insist their adaption honors some sort of inerrant, divine placement strategy.

In my own case, the "God doesn't make mistakes" argument falls short. I'm a nurse as well as a person of faith, and I've seen too many birth defects and congenital problems to assume that God's will is automatically in force for every body that opens the womb. Yes, God knows me from the womb and has a perfect plan for me; however, in this sinful world there are many pollutants, diseases, traumas, and disabling lifestyles that can disrupt the perfect plan on a fetal level (let alone during our development after birth). I think the "all-powerful" doctrine of God gets pushed beyond all reason, making us ask, "Why didn't God just stop this, or that, disaster?" or "Didn't God want me to be born with a hearing impairment?"

God doesn't make mistakes, but God's creation suffers nonetheless. The cross is an awful reminder of the lengths to which the Divine Spirit has gone to heal what is broken away from a perfect plan gone awry. And one of the ways we are most like God is the capacity to join God in the divine healing of our world and ourselves. For some, this is to embrace a "third gender," which God created in them. For me, it is to utilize all the tools currently available to embrace the reality my heart insists was God's original and final plan for me. God, being all-powerful in the sense that this power will eventually defeat the powers arrayed against the Plan, has given me the freedom to go a long way toward matching my inside with my outside.

I prayed: "Right or wrong, I must go this way, and would the Good Shepherd please follow me to help me be the best daughter of God I could be?" I firmly believe my prayer has been answered affirmatively.

Sadly, I have double standards just like most human beings. While I can say all these accepting things, I still wouldn't want to date or marry someone with a fluctuating gender identity. I've always seen men as the opposite sex and really enjoy them being men, frustrating as that is sometimes! Friendships with someone on a gender teeter-totter are one thing for me, an intimate relationship is quite another.

Is there a scriptural basis for ssexual reassignment surgery (SRS)? That is a challenge, but how about Matthew 18:7–9, which says, "Woe to the world because of stumbling blocks! Occasions for stumbling are bound to come, but woe to the one by whom the stumbling block comes! If your hand or your foot causes you to stumble, cut it off and throw it away; it is better for you to enter life maimed or lame than to have two hands or two feet and be thrown into the eternal fire. And if your eye causes you to stumble, tear it out and throw it away; it is better for you to enter life with one eye than to have two eyes and be thrown into the hell of fire." By the way, I find it pertinent that this is inserted right after Jesus' teaching about receiving the little child and is followed by a stern injunction not to despise "one of these little ones." As Jesus clearly teaches: "It is not the will of my Father who is in heaven that one of these little ones should perish." The full context is Matthew 18:1–14.

It was not my eyes, hands, or feet that caused me to live a life that was a lie. Pretending to be a man, in obedience to my body, was a temptation to deny the creative act of God in making my spirit female. Of course, SRS is not as simple as "cutting something off and throwing it away." This is not simply a subtractive procedure but involves creation as well. Nonetheless, this scripture resonates with me.

Had SRS not been done, I am fairly sure my condition could have been fatal—to my spirituality, my sanity, and even my physical body. There are way too many transgender men and women who commit suicide because they are convinced that they are acting against God's will. Now, read verse Matthew 18:14 and verses 5 and 6 over again. Who is in the shakier spot: the one who moves toward "the knife" or the one who rejects a child of God from coming before the Father?

Candidly, I wasn't sure I was right to continue toward SRS. As I said earlier, I prayed: "God, I might be wrong about who and what I am, but I HAVE to go there. Please walk with me and make me the best woman I can be, the one you wanted to create when you called me into life." I am now eleven years post-op and my stepdaughter just made me a grandmother. I always longed to be able to get pregnant; although that is impossible, I have a growing family.

God is not done with me yet. I believe that God does walk with me and has answered my prayer. The lessons Paul learned when he was sent to preach and baptize at the house of the Gentile, Cornelius (Acts 10), apply here. I refuse to say that what God has blessed is a lie or in any way apart from divine intention, and I really wish no one else would either. Let's leave the millstone for the mill!

19

THE BODY
SITE FOR THE DIVINE

LEWIS CHRISTOPHER PAYNE

RECOVERING THE INTEGRATION of body, soul, spirit, gender identity, and sexuality is a vital part of my journey towards wholeness. Reclaiming the passion of being a human person with a human, yet divine body has been central to my journey as a transgender person. Many of us, regardless of gender identity or sexuality, have complicated relationships with our bodies. Many of us to a greater or lesser extent experience discomfort being inside our own skin.

In my own experiences as a transgender person, coming back to my body and making peace with my body has been the most fundamental part of my transition and my faith journey of recent years. The body, my body, my imperfect body, that I would still wish to change has become the site of the Divine.

Let me explain what I mean. At the heart of this new relationship with myself is the incarnation: Jesus becomes flesh; Jesus becomes a human person; Jesus lives in a body; Jesus, in all his divinity, experiences life in a human body. Our physical selves bring us into communion with God and with each other. It is through our bodies that we physically experience the world, relationships with others, and the joys of intimacy. The fragility and the strength of our bodies is the essence of our humanity, sensations, and vulnerability.

For me and for many, discomfort with our physical bodies is one of the first signs of our transgender identity. As I grew up I became more aware of my body, and how that it did not seem to fit with the image I had of myself. I was in conflict with my body, the very place that I wanted to feel most at home. For me, survival meant disconnection. And this worked. Living a life disconnected from my body was costly, but it worked. Well, for a while at least, then the costs outweighed the benefits. It made me sick. I had to change, and I began to look for what was the matter. It took me a long time to find out what was the matter, but it was this journey that brought me into a relationship with God, and through which my faith came. My relationship with the church has not been so smooth—unfortunately at times God and God's people do not seem to be on the same wavelength.

However, for the last eight years of this journey, I have found a place where I can reconcile myself to my body, as well as to God. I found a place where my faith does not run at odds with my experience as a transgender person. Discovering a gospel of love and acceptance for all people—even me—has brought me back to the roots of my faith.

I have discovered the spiritual heart of living a gender variant life. Opening the pages of scripture and finding stories of myself has transformed my feelings about myself.

There are a few that are favorites of mine—the Ethiopian eunuch is perhaps the most obvious—a transgender person founding what has become the church in Africa. Then there are all the other eunuchs throughout the Bible, who pop up in important places carrying the story. Here I am doing quite a post-modern, queer reading of the Bible. But it makes sense to me. Who were eunuchs?—people born with different genitals, whom we would name as intersex people today, and people who became eunuchs, that is, were made so for their role in society, people we could name as transsexual people who change their bodies. Eunuchs were people who lived in gender roles other than the ones which their body might suggest. The expression "people who choose to become eunuchs," is often read as lesbian and gay people, but it can as easily be read as transgender people who change their outward gender presentation, but who might not have medical or surgical intervention.

Through this "transgender pair of spectacles" many characters in the Bible come alive as our spiritual ancestors—and as my friend George suggested, as our "trans-cestors."

And at the heart of it all you can find a gender variant water carrier who finds the upper room for the last supper. The disciples were asked by Jesus to look for a male water carrier—this seemingly insignificant fact has transformed the heart of my faith. Water carrying was traditionally a job done by women. So a male water carrier would be easy to spot in the crowds by the well on that day in Jerusalem, at Passover. In the throng the disciples looked for a male water carrier. This is amazing in and of itself. But then take a moment to think why this man might be a water carrier, why he might have a traditional female job. Could he have chosen this job because he felt more comfortable with a female role? Perhaps he identified himself as female? Or perhaps he used to identify himself as female, but now lives as male.

Just maybe the water carrier is a transgender person right at the heart of the story, which we do not even notice. Could he be a male-to-female person or a female-to-male person or an intersex person? It is speculative, but it is also not beyond the bounds of possibilities that this is one of our spiritual ancestors. Someone Jesus trusted enough to find them a place to gather at this busy time, when he could share those vital hours with his followers, the very time when he broke bread and they drank wine together. The very time when what is now communion was instigated—the body and the blood—that most intimate of meals that brings us into the most intimate communion with Jesus.

It is our bodies that bring us into communion with one another. The powerful symbolism of communion where we all share in Christ's body brings us together week after week. Jesus' body was broken, symbolically at the last supper and in reality on the cross. We as the body of Christ are made whole again when we take part in the communion meal. Communion is a healing act on a personal, social, and global level. There is something cosmically important about this meal. It heals the fabric of creation.

It is through communion that I, as a transman, find the wholeness that God has to offer.

20

SPIRITUAL DYNAMICS IN COMING OUT

AUDRA LYNN IMBODEN

NOT UNLIKE THE MAJORITY of us affected by gender dysphoria, my coming out presented itself as a very difficult period in life. If not for spirituality, I am convinced mine would have been a brief life. Although having been introduced to Jesus Christ in the fifth grade, having already been cross-dressing for a few years, I was unaware that a longing would gradually develop for knowing this Savior I had claimed to love. Little did I know my dissatisfaction with life would interrupt every other facet of my existence. By God's grace I managed to graduate from high school. But, while working in a factory, I was drafted by the army in June, 1966. I prayed earnestly that I would not be responsible for killing another human being. God granted my request. Although I served only two years, my specialized training kept me from doing any reserve duty for the remaining four years.

It was another three years, 1971, before I would learn the terminology describing the phenomenon I knew only as cross-dressing. Upon reading another transsexual's story in a large tabloid, I learned of the Erickson Educational Foundation. Writing to them, I received the advisory pamphlet "Legal Aspects of the Transsexual." Upon my initial attempt to secure assistance through local physicians, I became convinced I couldn't live with this. In response, I went down to our shed and hanged myself. Stepping off the five gallon bucket, the rope burned into my neck and then snapped. Falling to the ground, laughing frantically, I was overcome with the awareness that God was not going to allow me to get out of life without more struggles. A few days later I received a letter from a concerned physician who eventually assisted me in beginning hormone therapy—one who would eventually become instrumental in helping many peers in Northeast Indiana and the tristate area.

Soon, I was developing physically in a way I previously thought impossible, but I was cognizant of a lack of development that was beyond the material—I longed for that spiritual connection God has placed in each of us. Disconnected from the community of faith for quite some time, my spirit was exceedingly restless, and for resolve I sought involvement with and acceptance from members of the Church.

The congregation I was raised in moved from the inner city to its outskirts, worshipping in a gymnasium, and that did not appeal to me. Christmas of 1972 came like a flood—unemployment, living at home with my parents, their incapacity to understand why I wanted to be daughter number three, and a seventeen-year-old brother who was convinced I was homosexual. I sought outside solace, beyond the realm and scope of doctors and psychologists. With that deluge came my incessant desire to return to worshipping Christ. So on Christmas Eve I attended a service at a large inner-city Lutheran church. It was a candlelight service throughout which I sobbed—the beauty of the hour and the season mingled with the awareness of my own despair—my isolation in being transsexual in a midwestern hick town.

My parents had talked before Christmas of selling our home and land (twelve acres) to pay for a new house that we would construct ourselves. Having studied architecture, I was asked to design it. It was early 1973 and my assertiveness as a woman was growing, but so was that hunger for God and involvement in spiritual community. I decided to visit the edifice I once called my church. It had by then become occupied by a new congregation, but also made up of satellite families from other Lutheran congregations, who, for a prescribed period of time would strive together to establish a presence of Christ in that part of the city. I visited one Sunday, and then the following Sunday, and soon had several members asking why I wouldn't consider becoming a member.

Experiencing comfort in their presence week after week, my desire to become a member made its way to the pastor and congregational president. However, they realized that I was different than most people—most women—and that warranted a probe into my personal life, as some folks were asking questions about the type of person I presented. Subsequently, the pastor and a pastor/professor from the local Lutheran college came to visit my home prior to our moving. Although I was twenty-five, they were compelled to speak with my parents, to be certain that this was not some whim of sexual expression, but was what I had declared—what most of us have heard, and said ourselves—"I was a woman trapped in a man's body." These pastors stated they believed I knew Christ personally, and they apparently were satisfied with my parents' reasoning and acknowledgement that I was genuine in my beliefs. Not long thereafter during a special session of the church presbytery, I was in fact voted in as a member in good standing of Shepherd of the City Lutheran Church.

Such was my first encounter with a Body of Christ that was by all intents and purposes open and affirming long before I would first hear the term in context. There I once again connected with spiritual community, loved in my brokenness, yet allowed to reciprocate through the pouring out of her love for those whose fragmented lives were more easily concealed. Together, with no hidden agendas, we shared our lives through the life that is in Christ Jesus.

21

SELECTED POEMS

LESLIE WALTER

A LIFE WITHIN A LIFE

Like some Eastern mystic, I see
a wheel within a wheel
and in the battle
between body and soul, I see
a life within a life.

We harbor a changeling soul,
a love child adored, but hidden.
Until her strength
matches our own
and demands release.
Until endurance ends, and

laboring in the storm,
we become our own mothers
bringing forth
what is both self
and not-self.

But being your own child
means the line
between Old and New
is very thin.
A knife edge of pain
separates the two,
often forever,
condemning to oblivion
all that is good in the past.

Our mothers first saw us,
laid upon an empty belly
in ritual to soothe
the Old and the New,
re-establish the bond
broken in pain,
but needed still
for the nurturing to come.

We need a rite of our own
so we can live together
and choose a new course
amid the dying winds of pain.

LOVE COMES AND GOES

Like a joker in the night
love comes and goes
rearranging my life
taking up my time
tracking down the things
I had so neatly put away.

(UNTITLED)

There are no limits
on the dreams of children.
Young minds follow soaring hearts
until we teach them otherwise.

There are no limits
on the minds of grownups
if the child's heart survives.

INSIDE OUT

Trapped by expectations
I kept the best of me hidden
and shushed her when she spoke.

(UNTITLED)

Taking me where the trading's done
of one life for another,
and every choice we've ever made,
is labeled with its consequence.

With charts and graphs that demonstrate
the ups and downs of life,
that *shows* us how our dreams will change
and how we'll feel tomorrow.

22

THE RIGHT CHOICE FOR ME

JENNIFER LINDA BROOKS

MY NAME IS JENNIFER LINDA BROOKS. It took me thirty-eight years to be able to state that. I am a post-op transsexual woman. I had my surgery September 5, 2002, in Thailand by Dr. Preecha. I am now almost completely healed physically, mentally, and spiritually. I must say that its not an easy thing to start life over again not only physically, but emotionally and spiritually.

I was born October 28, 1963, as Joseph Pritula. My family was Roman Catholic. I grew up in a middle-class Italian family. Worse of all I was the only son! But you see, my brain kept telling me I was really the youngest daughter. I knew since I was five that I was not supposed to be male. I knew, but my family didn't. They had clues, such as my cross-dressing, playing with my sister's dolls, and hanging out with girls instead of boys. Deep down, they knew.

More importantly, I knew. Growing up Catholic and as a so-called "boy," I really had a problem with faith! I had gone through baptism as a baby, as most did, but communion was another matter. Communion was one of the moments of my life when I knew that I should have been with the girls rather than the boys. Communion is when you are supposed to grow closer to God and learn about your place in the church. You are supposed to be able to confess your sins to the priests as if you are confessing to God. How's that for conflict! Here I was dying to tell everyone that I was not really a boy. I even tried once to bring it up with a religious sister—a nun (a more liberal sister, or so I thought)—who taught me in Sunday school. She told me, "If God wanted you to be a girl he would have made you one." I never forgot that! For years I thought that my impulse to be female was a curse. I blamed myself and I blamed God! I remember thinking, why did you make me feel like this? Why do I have to carry this cross and masquerade as a boy? Why, God, why?

I grew further from the church as I grew up. Even though I went to church every Sunday with family, I was just going through the motions. Confirmation, another Catholic ritual, was even worse for me. First I had to choose a new name, a Catholic name, for my confirmation in heaven. A male name! I remember that everyone had already had their name but me, as I just didn't and couldn't think of one that would suit me. Kathryn and Mary were not acceptable. I do remember that the father took me aside and finally started to convince me to take Michael. So I did. Even worse, while most girls had a godmother, I had to choose a godfather. Actually my mother chose my uncle for me—a man I despised. I hated the whole ceremony and promised myself that I would never have the two other important Catholic rituals—marriage and last rites!

A Catholic upbringing for a transsexual is not easy. The Catholic Church doesn't understand or believe in transgender expression. In the church's eyes I am sinning and being homosexual. The same church that taught against sin and debauchery would later be sued for the same debauchery. Ironic, yet very poetic. All this drove me away from God and organized religion.

For years I didn't believe in God. The final straw was when my father killed himself and left me in charge as the "man" of the family. Now it seemed as if my destiny was sealed. I was very far from God now. I not only hated myself and the lie that I was portraying, but I hated God for giving me this cross to bear. Once my family was taken care of so that I could leave the area and be on my own, I was on a mission to destroy my-self. I fell into drugs and a fast lifestyle for a while. I bent a few laws and did some things I am not proud of. It's amazing that I wasn't killed or put into jail for some of it. I even thought about ending it all.

At this point in my life I was without any faith and just wanted the nightmare to end. I tried to convince myself that I really was male and that my "femaleness" was just a habit that I could control. I joined the military at this point. I figured the army could make a man out of me or I could end up getting killed. Either way, my problem would be solved. Going into the military was really tough, as again it demonstrated that I was not one of the guys. It seemed the more I tried to be a guy the more the girl in me grew. I was so miserable and tried on a few occasions to drink myself to death. I volunteered to go to dangerous places and even took airborne training. I suppressed myself so much that I fooled myself into believing that I was forced to be a man forever. I'm sure God was with me at times because I had some close calls where I really did believe I was going to die, but I lived and felt cheated. Finally, I left the military and decided to try to be a guy and live my life.

I came home from my time in service and made the mistake of lis-tening to my family and getting a job and trying to settle down. My mother wanted grandchildren so I tried dating women. All my life I have always felt something for men, not women. Men always melted my heart even though I hid it. I only wanted a man to take me and love me as a woman. It never worked out that way; now I would try to be the guy and find a woman for me.

It was a joke, as I could never perform as a normal boyfriend and none of the relationships I tried would work. Giving yourself to someone is as personal as it gets. I never considered myself homosexual, yet being with women didn't work, as I just couldn't be the man. Again I thought about myself and my situation. I knew who I was. I had known since childhood that I was transsexual. Now I was thirty-five and a complete failure as a man.

One night I went on a long drive and took my gun and almost ended it all. I was so tired of hating the whole life I had. I drank bourbon and drove to an empty field somewhere in north Florida. I drank and tried to summon up the courage. I tried and I tried but I couldn't do it. There was a voice calling, from inside and above, "Don't kill me!" I ended up waking up in my truck that morning very hung over. I drove home and went to bed and that's when I had a great dream. I don't remember it! It was that great. What I do remember is waking up in a cold sweat with one thing running through my mind: "Butterflies have to be free." I stood up, I went to the mirror, and I made a choice. I was done being miserable. I was done lying. I was done living my life for others. Now I live for me.

I decided to find a psychotherapist. I decided to open up and tell him all about me. He referred me to a specialist in gender. After seeing her for a few visits, I could see that she had planned to string me along, to be a gatekeeper, so to speak. Again I decided that no one would decide for me. At this time I began to build my faith again. As I started transition on my own, I decided that I would leave all of the past behind. I started to believe more in destiny and that now I was finally on the right trail.

I know my church didn't understand, but not all of us are the same. We have diversity and it's all around us. It's what makes us human. I started to reread the Bible and research Jesus' life as I researched my own transition and discovered that there are similarities.

Jesus had to take a path that he didn't want to take (but did) and his life was about teaching love and humanity. I feel now that I am on a path, and it's a gift rather than a curse. I have taken off my mask and am living my life as myself. I am transsexual, and now I no longer have to conceal it. I have come to understand who I am now and why I am. Because I know who I am I also know that there is a higher power guiding me. I have invited God back into my life. I'm almost ready to join the church again as I am healing. I have found a church that I believe is about love and understanding, MCC (Metropolitan Community Church) in Sarasota. I believe I have found church again. The prodigal daughter returns.

I have made the choice that I shall, with God's help, teach humanity and understanding to the ignorant. Remember, acceptance begins with understanding. I feel the choices we make in life are what bring us closer to God! Now I feel I am living! The right choice for me! Praise God!

23

SPIRITUAL JOURNEY

CHRISTINE LOVELESS

EARLY IN THE YEARS OF MY TRANSITION, I was searching for a place of worship that would accept me and be within traveling distance. I had been a member of the United Methodist Church since childhood. Many of my family members are Methodist ministers. During a search, I found a United Methodist Church that was open to gays and lesbians. That church was a great distance from home. A Metropolitan Community Church, openly "reaching beyond gay and lesbian community," was close but the service time was inconvenient.

By reading an editorial, I discovered a church. Pastor Kathy wrote the editorial, "Homophobic acts show need for hate-crime laws." I arranged an appointment to discuss the church with her. We were both open regarding my transition. I felt satisfied that I had discovered a church home, a friendly Presbyterian church.

As I grew in my transition to be a part of society, I needed a community that was not all gay and lesbian. I did not want a place of worship that preached "love the person, hate the sin." I did want a place of worship that truly accepted a mixture of worshipers. I wanted a group open to education and discussion about transgender topics. Likewise, I wanted a minister who was comfortable discussing injustice and hatred along with love and acceptance. I wanted to ask the worshippers, "Are we to follow the church or Jesus' method of teaching and acceptance?"

Kathy preached about loving people who are different and was very aware of the use of gender neutral language and so much more. I knew Kathy lived what she preached through her attitude toward her gay son. She blended her sermons to be candid and straightforward, based on an open and thorough understanding of the scripture.

Kathy moved to Nebraska to be closer to her family in Colorado. I was very fond of her and I miss her dearly. After she left at one service, the clergy person spoke about a man who loves a man. I was upset to hear that he cannot become a full-time minister because he is gay. Is it necessary to be straight in order to teach the love of Jesus?

Lately, I have not been at church. I am going through an inner struggle dealing with people who are not open-minded. I would just like to see the church teach the way Jesus did. Jesus interacted with a variety of people and did not turn anyone away. I believe there is one standard—accept Jesus into your heart.

I have accepted Jesus into my heart. It is a great feeling to know that there is someone who loves people who are different. If you are struggling with the church's method, I hope you accept Jesus into your heart. In addition to my transgendered issues, I also have a learning disability.

Although I can blend with society, I can sense insensitivity towards people who are different. I am willing to educate and to discuss transgender topics with anyone who is open-minded. I am, however, weak in communication skills, which hinders my discussion. I can relate with transgenders who would like to share their experiences and who are concerned about how their experiences will be received.

24

TRANSCENDING PHYSICAL BOUNDARIES AND SICK RELIGION
THE STORY OF A TRANSSEXUAL MYSTIC

ASHLEY MOORE

MY NAME IS ASHLEY MOORE and what follows is as much a testimony about the growth of my faith as it is a statement of how I came to my transition as a transsexual being. Until just a few years ago my life felt like one endless story of shame and suffering. But in my darkest hour, I was able to confront my worst fears; to face the truth of who I am; and, in so doing, to finally bring all of myself to God. It was only then that I could finally heal.

I was the child of a violent, alcoholic father and a codependent mother who both grew up under repressive Christian doctrine. The product of racially mixed marriages, I experienced racism from within and without my family. We were poor and spent half of my childhood on welfare. We were forced to move so often that by the time I was eighteen, I had lived in sixteen different places. I have been beaten, kicked, thrown, burned, choked, cut, shot at, and told daily that I was a flawed useless mistake that would never amount to anything. The neglect at home was so bad that I once had a terrible fever, was unconscious and delirious for nearly four days, and no one in my family called a doctor or even checked my temperature. I was so unhappy that at the age of only six, I made my first attempt to commit suicide. Eventually, I became a runaway, a homeless addict, a felon, a sexual user, and a suicide risk who was finally abandoned and ostracized by my family. As a result of all this, I never felt like I belonged *anywhere*. I never had a sense of home or of community and never had any real friends until I was fifteen. I had come to believe that God was making me suffer because I *was* abhorrent. The reason? Ever since I was four years old, I felt that I was supposed to be a female.

When I was really young, I just believed that was who I was, what I would grow up to be. By the time I was eight, I realized that something wasn't right, as I was being told that I was a boy and had to behave certain ways. My father (who it turns out was struggling with his transgendered feelings), even tried to beat my femininity out of me. My classmates teased me and called me "sissy" and "faggot" no matter what school I attended. And while I was certain that what they were accusing me of (being attracted to males) was inaccurate, I had an increasing awareness that I was different. But with all the turmoil in my family life, the issue was obscured by other circumstances. So I would sit quietly in my grade school classes longing to be one of the girls and not understanding why I felt this way.

By the time I was nearly ten years old, my mother and I had a discussion that would change my life for twenty years. I was asking her why my father was so angry and why he had been institutionalized for a while. She told me that he was "very sick" and had been questioning his sexuality, and that he had sometimes dressed in women's clothing. She went on to say that she was going to use this information against him in their divorce because "that type of behavior is an abomination in God's eyes." Effectively, she communicated that feeling gender conflicted was wrong, offensive, a sickness, and a sin that was worthy of public humiliation and abandonment by loved ones. On that day, I began twenty years of denial and a struggle to be loved by a God who I believed would not accept my flawed nature.

From that day on I tried to act more masculine. I spent months working on my walk, trying to adopt a tougher exterior. I tried to be less emotive, more reserved in exchanges, and more aggressive in sports. By the time I was in junior high school I was already well versed in hiding my pain and sadness. I was doing my best to fit in and not feel like a freak because of all that our little family had been through, the upheaval and unsettledness. We were all trying to get on with our lives. Of course no one knew that I was growing more confused and afraid about the things I was feeling.

My father's daily beratement of my value as a human being and constant reminders that I was a mistake only fueled this state of mind. By the time I was a senior in high school, I had come to believe that these feelings were proof positive that my father was right. I used to beg God to make me stop feeling this way, to make me normal and not to forsake me. The effects of abandonment, violence, and alcoholic-fueled codependent behavior of my family all served to reinforce this denial as well. Driving all this fear in me was the simple need to be loved and not rejected by my family.

By the time puberty began, I was already well into denial. I had always found females attractive and this became both affirming and confusing. I couldn't be gay, after all, if I liked girls. But I still wanted to *be* a girl. Eventually I began to wonder, "How do I know I'm not gay?" All the guys in my school seemed so sure I was—maybe I was and didn't know it. So I experimented with boys as well, but it didn't feel right.

Meanwhile my relationships with females were distressing. The girls would treat me as one of their best friends, which was fantastic. But the moment something romantic or sexual would happen, the energy between us would shift and polarize and I would find them placing masculine role expectations on me that would make me run. And as my body began to change, I felt betrayed even by my body.

At some point I learned what a transvestite was   meaning a sexual deviant—and it made me nauseated! This was never a sexual thing with me. But there was no other information available to me that would describe what I felt. So where did all this leave me? A) I didn't feel like a male, I felt like a girl; B) I wasn't attracted to males, but females, and; C) I didn't have a fetishistic involvement with women's clothes, but dressed like one on the rare occasion that I could and then would apologize to God and beg God's forgiveness.

As a result, I was a teenager who was lost and out of control. I had an arrest record; ran away from home; sought solace in sex and all manner of illegal substances; and parented a child with a girl who didn't love me, all while filling books and tapes with my own songs about what I was going through. I was desperately depressed and struggling with gender issues.

Although my years as a drummer provided a visceral outlet for my distress, it was only when I picked up the guitar and began writing songs at the age of thirteen that I began articulating my inner turmoil. As my need to find solace in music grew, I discovered that the persona of a "musical artist" gave the people around me a way of accepting my "otherness." I could be sensitive, emotive, and even vulnerable. I could wear my hair long, wear brighter colored clothing, and distance myself from the "jocular" pursuits of my male peers. So I began crafting another layer of false masculine identity in order to just be accepted.

My need to be "normal," to fit in, and to be loved informed most of my decisions. My eagerness to land in a stable and long-term relationship with a female at seventeen was a part of this. It was then that I met the woman who became my partner of fifteen years and who was the daughter of two Unitarian ministers. To not have my sexuality questioned any longer was remarkable. To have the intimacy in which to grow and be supported was a dream come true. But all along I kept thinking "maybe this will make me feel like a man and make these feelings stop." I even thought that on my wedding day: "Perhaps it finally ends here."

The Unitarian church, and the Universalist ideology, had presented a new way of understanding spirituality. Since I believed I would never be good enough for Christ, I spent the next ten years looking for a belief system where I could have a personal relationship with God. I studied the major religions as well as various mystical and indigenous practices. Still, I did not find a way to have the experience of the Divine that I knew was possible. It took me many more years to realize that it was the belief that God could not love me that prevented me from having the intimacy I longed for.

Meanwhile, my early adulthood only served to make me more convinced of my damnation. By nineteen, both sets of my parents had disowned me. I was broke and living at the heart of one of the worst ghettos in the Bay Area, and, after inadvertently becoming mixed up with gangsters, had a price on my head. During the same year, I watched Child Protective services tear the remainder of my family apart, which led in short order to my father's suicide.

At this point I turned to my music full time. Music had been an outlet for me through all the traumas of my life. In it I found my only emotional comfort, a source of true joy and my sense of connection to the Divine. In 1989, I wrote a poem that included the line: "I lose myself in you, my dearest music; the only constant of my life. My therapist, friend, and lover who has never turned on me." I reasoned that if God had given me the talent to perform, compose, and "capture" music, it would be through this anointing that I would find my way into God's grace.

The one advantage to relocating frequently was that I had been presented with many different opportunities to use my talents and was fortunate to perform with award-winning vocal ensembles, drama departments, and jazz and marching bands at statewide competitions. After I moved to Boston and put myself through music college, I toured the United States playing guitar and singing in a nine-piece funk/R&B/world music group. Later, I became the production manager of a nightclub showcasing national acts. I was also staff engineer at several recording studios. Before long my name was on records all over the world and I was flying to New York and Los Angeles, shopping acts, and negotiating record deals with some of the most powerful people in the music industry. I had my own studio business, a house, two cars, a dog, and a "successful" fifteen-year relationship. But in my heart, I was miserable. In 1993 my first "out" experience exploring my transgendered self had led to my being raped. This turned into a situation where I was blackmailed into maintaining contact with this individual, which invariably led to further sexual abuse. This experience seemed to affirm my fear that such expressions of my feminine identity could only lead to evil.

In the meantime, I had gotten on the Internet. For a very short period in 1996, I began assuming a feminine persona and was surprised to find that there were other people who had these feelings too. In short order, I chatted with some of these people, learned the terms transgendered and cross-dresser, and for the first time in my life I realized that the word transsexual had some relationship to myself. It scared me to death! It conjured up all my fears of abandonment and ostracism. I stopped going online and began the most intense period of denial in my life. But that information had caused a permanent fissure in my reality.

Whenever I stopped working, my brain would turn to these unanswered questions about gender identity. So finally I stopped having an emotional life at all; I began working nonstop (sixteen hours a day, seven days a week for over two years), stopped going home most nights, and only found "peaceful" sleep by drinking myself to sleep. And every single day I wrestled with the idea of suicide. I never felt farther from God. In those years, I began to long to achieve success and wealth, for I had been deceived into thinking that I could use my talent to earn enough money that I could buy my way out of despair. I began looking for freedom in my golden calf. But God was about to make a way.

In the last months of 1997, I was working on a gospel record with some clients at my studio. As the recordings progressed and these mighty singers sang their heartfelt praises, I again found myself longing to know God. By chance, one of these sessions was cancelled, which allowed my wife and I a rare, spontaneous date. We went to the UC Theater in Berkeley to see a film. I grabbed the listing of upcoming movies for the theater. A movie titled, "Let Me Die a Woman" caught my eye. The description said something about "a documentary following the lives of three transsexual women, which features rare footage of a sex change operation." When the day came, I went to see that move.

In spite of the drawbacks to the movie, when I walked out of the theater I understood for the first time in my life, "I *am* a transsexual." I sat in my car for an hour and cried my eyes out. Suddenly everything made sense and I knew that my life would never be the same. I went home and prayed and said to God, "Lord, you know I have been fighting this my whole life and I have begged you for twenty years to make me stop feeling this way. But Lord, if this is the truth, if this is the way I am supposed to be, then I need you to show me the way. You will have to lead the way. I will trust in you to see me through." At last I faced the truth of who I have always been and was finally able to bring all of myself before God. That very day, for the first time in my life, I felt the Lord God comfort and lead me. And God has been leading me ever since.

Very quickly I realized that I needed to get into specialized therapy. I began researching the subject of transgender with every spare moment I had. To my relief, most of the first things I found were related to being a transgendered Christian—I was so thankful for the guidance and began to praise God from the depths of my being. Within three weeks, I had begun therapy, told two close friends what was going on, and began preparing myself to tell my wife.

She took it really well—we held each other and cried all night. "It all makes sense now, everything fits," she murmured. "We'll try to get through this together." And to her credit, she did try her best to be okay with it and make it work. But in her own ways, she was just as stuck as I was and her personal growth limited by the boundaries of our relationship. Finally, we realized that the best thing for both of us was to leave the marriage. We are still good friends.

But even before that, it wasn't long before things began to unravel for me, as things do for people who've been living a lie for so long. I had to deal with my denial and all the unhealthy choices I had made to get me there. As one writer puts it, "Sex is screwing. Everything else is gender." As I began to remember all the ways in which I had tried to masculinize myself out of fear and as I began to be aware of how gender roles inform everything we do, I began to have a major identity crisis. I was peeling back the layers of my shell, back down to that ten-year-old kid standing with Mom in the hospital that day. I felt I had finally found my inner child only to discover she was a scared little girl and that I had to grow up all over again. I finally found that I *had* to start making changes and begin telling people.

In that same time, I read the Bible and found that God in Christ was very different from the religion I had been taught. When I learned that the word homosexual first appeared in the Bible in 1946 and that the scriptures used against queers were mistranslated from the original texts, I began to realize that I had been given a distorted view of God. And once I saw that both the Hebrew and Christian texts affirmed eunuchs, that universal third gender in its many forms, I was freed from the prison that had been built out of other people's lies. Instead of feeling cursed, I began to feel blessed and became increasingly determined to spread these truths so that others will not suffer as I did.

As I transitioned, I found strength in God even as I lost everything I had worked so hard to achieve—the wife, the house, the business, etc. But even as it was coming down around me, I had hope for the first time in my life because I finally knew Christ and recognized that I too am wonderfully made in his image. I knew that his love for me was unconditional and that he would deliver me into his plan if only I would let him.

More than three years have passed since then. I have made many changes in my life, my body and social role. Today, I live "full time" as a woman. I am now legally and socially known as "Ashley Moore." I have changed my gender through a series of reassignment procedures following the American Medical Association's guidelines and current protocol for the treatment of chronic gender identity dysphoria, and now live as a female. I became a candidate for sex reassignment surgery in January of 2001.

More than this, I am extremely happy. Since I found the courage to begin taking the steps to face my truth, my life has opened in so many wonderful ways. In that time I have found a joy and inner peace that I had never known before—the kind of peace I had almost given up hope of ever experiencing. My transition has been a journey into my faith in God, and I am deeply spiritual as a result.

They say that happiness is not a destination, but a road by which you travel. You have to choose to be happy in your life. For me, accepting the truth about myself was the beginning of that choice. Giving my life to Jesus and surrendering to his will was the choice that set me free!

Just as my marriage ended and my grandfather was dying from leukemia, I was called into my first act of ministry. I helped him renew his faith, which allowed him to make his peace with the family, which in turn healed many wounds. That led to my first act of music ministry as I sang my grandfather's favorite hymn at his funeral: "How Great Thou Art." This song later became a powerful vehicle through which God's will for me has been confirmed. As I became active in the transgender community, I began to hear others talk about what they were going through and express how they felt abandoned by God. As I talked about my life, it helped others, particularly to find their way to God. Suddenly I began to thank God for all that I had happened in my life. I began to see how my suffering and my opportunities had been preparing me for ministry. As I began to ask for confirmation of this, I began to be led to places where I could find answers. I was called upon to share the word and the love of God, which led me a year later to my wonderful church, the City of Refuge.

God had been leading me strongly for a couple of weeks and it had built to a fever pitch in the days prior to going to my first service at Refuge. I'd had a profound series of conversations, revelations, and messages so that I was in a deep praise the night before. At that service on October 2, 2000, every single thing that was spoken or sung seemed to affirm all that I had been experiencing. And I was overwhelmed, because I had not dared believe such a church existed—an institution that reflected the God I had come to know. Yet here it was and I wept for sheer joy at the beauty of it. I felt like I had come home. Here was the spiritual community I had needed and searched for my whole life. It was one of the most powerful experiences I have ever had. In this church I have found the community I had never known. And I am so thankful for God's mercy and love that I still weep for joy at every service.

God was guiding me to create a music ministry for the transgender community. With the encouragement of people at the City of Refuge, this became a choir. As it turns out, the Transcendence Gospel Choir, an all-transgendered choir, is the first of its kind in the world. We sing praises and minister to transpeople about God's unconditional love. Transgendered persons seem to be an acutely spiritual people. Perhaps this is because once you reach the point of saying that who you are transcends your physical form, then you are immediately aware of yourself as a spiritual being. Maybe this is why transgender people throughout history have been closely associated with spiritual worship. Regardless, my goal is not to convert anyone to Christianity but rather to let those who have been driven from their faith know that God *does* love them for *who* they are, not what they call themselves or what they choose to wear. Jesus said simply "*whosoever* believes in me shall have everlasting life."

All of this has allowed me to face the world honestly and as a complete human being. I have been blessed to have most of my friendships deepen, to know greater love and compassion in all of my personal relationships, and to find genuine devotion and support in my professional relationships. I now live with my lesbian partner in Alameda, California, and work really hard to maintain a healthy union while enjoying life as much as we can. In the years ahead, I plan to move into ministry full-time and thereby give all of my life to serving God.

25

A LITTLE ALLITERATIVE LITERATURE OR AN ITTY BITTY GENDER DITTY

ANNA MAE CAROLYNE

I was at once struck by the notion—transcending gender . . .
    a gender transcender?
The notion is both frightening and enlightening,
but would it mean the ending of bending forth is old gender bender?

No dressing with gusto, no makeup, no frocks . . .
stuck with a suit, fly fronts, and green socks?

Yuck! sez this bender to ending the splendor.
"I don't like the idea of ending it here at transgender.

That's not what I bought
when I started this journey to seek and be sought.

Nay, nay, sez the guide—you have nothing to fear.
You may seek what is sought with one foot staying here."

"Do you mean, do you say—while I curiously peer
at Transcendence, I need not abandon what's true, near, and dear?

"So keep attending to bending, to gending and trending,
and sending and mending, and blending and amending.

"Transcending, you see, is not this or that.
It's a state of being, like wearing a hat.

"So keep bending thy gending keep lending thy ear
Keep listening and hoping for a happy new year.

If you bender your gender with no fear and great pride
then some day you'll make it to the great other side.

Part Three

WORSHIP RESOURCES AND BIBLE STUDIES

26

PRAYERS FOR CONGREGATIONAL USE

PRAYER OF CONFESSION

O God, you are both Father and Mother to us, yet we confess we are uncomfortable with those who don't fit our categories. Mystery frightens us. Arid reason resists ambiguity. Remind us that we are not created for regimentation but for gratitude. Help us claim our baptismal identity as children of God, disciples of Christ, members of the church, and then discover this baptismal gift in others, even those whose identities confound our assumptions. Thus may your church be an icon of your Triune life where difference constitutes unity and oneness is expressed in rich diversity. Amen.

—*Rev. John Thomas, General Minister and President, United Church of Christ*

PRAYER

God of many facets, you who transcend gender and history, time and space, the laundry and the mortgage, the carpool and the chaos, draw near. Open our hearts to each other, reduce our fear and prejudice. May transgendered people come to be at home in every community and may gender itself find its place in the annals of history as something wonderful, God-given, and as multifaceted as you and your creation. In the name of Jesus, who transcended gender himself. Amen.

—*Rev. Donna Schaper*

A PRAYER FOR COMING OUT AS TRANSGENDER

Creator God, I am learning things all the time. It is a gift to be young and to get to know you and your world, your beautiful creation. I am also getting to know myself, and I'm discovering that sometimes I feel as if I were the other gender. Sometimes I feel scared about these feelings. Sometimes I feel wonderful about them. I know that I am your creation, and you have given me a wonderful gift in my gender identity. I pray for your supporting presence as I become more comfortable with my feelings. I pray for your guidance, that I may know when it is the right time for me to let other people know about this part of me. I pray for your supporting presence if I should be rejected, knowing that you, God who created me, will not reject me, that you will affirm me as part of your beautiful creation. In you I trust. Amen.

Reprinted with permission from Leanne McCall Tigert and Timothy Brown, eds., Coming Out Young and Faithful, *(Cleveland: Pilgrim Press, 2001).*

PRAYER

Unswayable, redeeming God, you heal the incurable wound of Zion and restore health to injuries beyond healing.* Especially when no one cares and we are cast out, even should we come to believe we deserve abandonment due to some supposed sin, you do not renounce us. Our hearts cry for vengeance, but we refuse to copy the evil done to us by hating our haters.

Foil haters by dismantling hate, Mighty God. Revise wicked hearts, converting casters of stones into throwers of lifelines. Plunder their dark, little minds and steal away their sin. Exile the true public enemies, the demons of prejudice and scorn. Consummate Jesus' death for sin as the death of sin by converting us to love one another as He bid us. Christ pleads the cause of those with no worldly advocate and attends to the despair of the outcast. Like orbits of His prayers, may our lives revolve around divine love. Amen.

*(See Jer. 30: 12–17 and John 17.)

—*Rev. Sheryl Stewart*

A PRAYER OF GRATITUDE

Holy God,
I am most grateful to you for *voice* . . . mine.
Like the lapping of the wave upon hot summer sand
reminds me of your constancy,
Like thunder applauding your power and majesty,
Like prophets calling your people to justice and mercy and diversity,
Like Jesus was your sounding board and *being*.

Like the tinkling of mercy,
the bellowing of joy,
the murmur of secrets,
the clarity of story finally told.

I am most grateful to you for *voice*, nearly buried, burrowing and authentic.
Calling, calling, calling to be heard.

The medicine that lifted my adolescent song to treble clefs and discordant
cliffs is gone. Each morning, I joy with the ringing congruence of self and
sound. Deep rich male sonorous expressions surrounding and defining me.
Belly laughs of richness. Surprising power in a small room. Startling and
thrilling me simultaneously. I love to listen to *me*.

As your people know you by your *voice*, I, too, am known.
Intrinsically. Surely. Essentially.

I joy to hear *me* singing hymns, louder than *her* in the pew beside.
Melody, low and resonating. I whisper more loudly than intended.
I am startled by *my* own volume, apologizing, with glad heart, for this
irreverence.

O holy God, *voice* of all creation, melody of all beings, Script of the
living,
Thank you for this my Authentic voice. I just *love* it! Can you hear it?
Of course, you do!
Thanks and *amen*.

—*Pastor Judith Hanlon*

PRAYERS AT THE BEGINNING OR AT A SIGNIFICANT JUNCTION IN TRANSITION

1

God, these are instruments of your creativity—
hormone injections, electrolysis, surgery,
new clothes and new names—
We dedicate them to your blessing.

God, these are channels of your grace—
dear friends, therapists, doctors,
family members—honest with hope or doubt—
and a community of open-hearted love.
We dedicate them to your blessing.

May the valley of dry bones
be knit together into new body,
and, in the desert of spirit,
may the crocus of personality bloom.

You who promised Nicodemus that "born again"
was a real possibility, send your Holy Spirit
upon the transition of this your child _____.
Amen.

(Ezek. 37; Isa. 35; John 3)

2

God, who brings butterfly from chrysalis,
hyacinth from bulb,
resurrection from grave clothes—
tenderly open new life,
for your child _____,
that s/he may grow physically,
emotionally, and spiritually
into the new creation you intend him/her to be.
Amen.

—*Maren C. Tirabassi*

CONFESSION

God of the gentle yoke, God of the come-unto-me welcome,
as individuals in faith communities and as churches, we ask forgiveness
for those times we have ignored the boy in the girl,
and the girl in the boy,
for jokes about cross-dressing
harsh as vinegar on a sponge,
for facile assumptions that gender minorities
must somehow lack enough faith,
for standing in the grim lineage, all the way back
to Jesus' time, of religious people
who resented other people's healing
when it didn't follow protocol,
for calling unclean that which God has called clean,
judging with an eye-plank the size of a pew,
erecting stumbling blocks big as jersey barriers
before your weary and heavy-laden children
who are trying to come to you. Amen.
(Matt. 11: 28–30; Acts 10,11; Matt. 7:1–5; Mark 9:42)

—M. C. T.

CONFESSION

O God, we confess that we accept certain life changes and conversions,
and deny others.
We rejoice with alcoholics and addicts when they take the first step.
We celebrate those who—in the excitement of the revival tent
or the solitude of midnight contemplation—
pray the prayer that changes everything.
We give thanks for those who are called to ministry, mission, advocacy.
And yet we fear, question, and deny the gender-converted,
suggesting that they are mistaken or need more time.
Strip away, O God, our layers of hypocrisy
and lead us, like Ananias visiting Paul,
to a place of support, affirmation, and rejoicing
for all those you convert, transform, and give new life. Amen.
(Acts 9:10–19)

—M. C. T.

PRAYER FOR A TRANS-WELCOMING CHURCH

God, teach us to be a trans-welcoming church.
Help women welcome new women and men welcome new men—
setting aside the stereotypes of attractiveness
the harsh little insider-rules of appearance.
Help all of us welcome people who dwell in both worlds—
by making smooth the rough places,
especially gender divided restrooms,
activities, liturgies, clubs, and traditions.
Help us to listen. Amen

—*M. C. T.*

PRAYER AT A FUNERAL

God, we acknowledge at this time of passing
that this was one of your children
who experienced both sorrow and joy
[*add other emotions that are appropriate, such as
anxiety, persecution, celebration, or alienation*]
because of her/his need to stand before you with integrity.

Now s/he has come to the dimension called resurrection,
promised by Jesus Christ to be beyond all such divisions.
Now there is not male and female.
Now our friend _____ is like an angel of God.
This body, like a seed, has fallen to the ground
and rises up a spiritual body—imperishable and immortal.
For this new great mystery we give you thanks. Amen.

(Matt. 22:30; 1 Cor. 15:35–58)

—*M. C. T.*

**PRAYER FOR CHANGING AN OPEN AND AFFIRMING STATEMENT
TO REFLECT TRANSGENDER ISSUES**

Read 2 Corinthians 4:7.

God, we are aware that all our words are clay pots.
This morning we break and remake
our Open and Affirming Statement
to clearly welcome your transgender children,
as well as those who are gay, lesbian, and bisexual.

We recognize that we will never fully hold
in our words the wideness of your love.

Bless our attempt to open our hearts and our church,
and bless each person who will experience hospitality—
not our hospitality, but the hospitality of Jesus Christ,
who blesses the joy and fragility of human bodies
through the wonder of the incarnation. Amen.

—*M. C. T.*

PRAYERS USING BIBLICAL IMAGES

1

God, we are people of the rib.
We are your transgender children
who know male and female—
both sides of your glorious image.

We experienced life as deep sleep
until you came to us,
until you brought redefinition
out of us—flesh of our flesh.

The tearing out of a rib hurts.
We hurt. But we also bloom —
with a garden-full of blessing
and the joy of naming ourselves.
Amen.

(Gen. 1, 2)

2

God, we are your transgender children.
We are wine in the water pots—pour us.
We were grave-wrapped and stone sealed
by loving family—Lazarus-us forth
newly alive in their presence.
We come night-sneaking to you
like Nicodemus,
not quite believing in born-again.

Startle us into a miracle,
by looking into our faces
and recognizing who we are. Amen.

(John 2, John 11, John 3)

3

Christ, just as you were mistaken for the gardener
by Mary Magdalene's love,
so we are not recognized by those
who loved us before our transition.

As you spoke gently to her,
but did not allow her to cling and hold you,
so help us define ourselves
with absolute clarity but without anger.

Teacher, Savior, Risen One,
help us to rise, and then guide us forth
from the garden. Amen.

(John 20:11–18)

4

God, my life is tossed like a storm
and this frail fishing boat, my body,
does not steer by the compass in my brain.
It seems like you are asleep and do not care
whether I drown under waves of depression and despair,
or crash on the rocks of intolerance and bigotry.
Savior—wake up and control this storm.
As you did so long ago in Galilee, say,
"Peace, be still." Amen.

(Mark 4:35–41)

5

God, like Joseph in Potiphar's house, sometimes we run out of our clothes
in order to keep our integrity. Like David facing Goliath, sometimes we
need to choose our own garments and weapons rather than wearing the
unwieldy armor society hands us. Like Esther in her younger days, some-

times we need a long process of cosmetic change to prepare us for our destiny. Keep us safe and certain; help us find love and support; remind us that, even when we see ourselves in a mirror dimly, you see us face to face. Amen.

(Gen. 39; 1 Sam. 17: 38–40; Esth. 2:5–11; 1 Cor. 13:12)

6

God, I am like the demoniac healed by Jesus' mercy and strength. I feel like I've lived in the graveyard of my possibilities, breaking society's chains but then hurting myself with the sharp stones of self-hatred and despair. Send the legion of my fears, doubts, and self-criticisms over the cliff and return me home in my right mind and self. Then, Savior, help my home-folks receive me and help me be patient with their too-obvious cautions, mixed feelings, and nervous mistakes in hospitality. Amen.

(Mark 5:1–20)

7

God, the pumpkin doesn't look like the pumpkin seed, nor the marigold like the marigold seed, the oak like the acorn, the spruce like the cone, the hyacinth like the bulb, the chick like the egg, the frog like the tadpole. Natural to your world is a dramatic change in life. Some of your children are so transformed. We have changed dramatically. We give thanks for that mystery, even as it foreshadows the time when, for all of us, the perishable is imperishable, the mortal, immortal and we each are raised up as spiritual bodies through the victory of our Savior Jesus Christ. Amen.

(1 Cor. 15:35–57)

8

God, you are the potter. Hold your hand upon our spinning on the wheel of life and remake us into a vessel, a body, that is pleasing to you, that is, indeed, your original and most holy intention for us. Help us to become prophets of the Potter and proclaim to others that we hold our truths in fragile clay vessels and that it is your will to spin all your creations to be useful and beautiful, rather than breaking the cup with no handle or the vase that cannot hold a flower and throwing the pieces away. Amen.

(Jer. 18:1–4; Isa. 64:8; 2 Cor. 4:7)

—M. C. T.

27

RESOURCES FOR AN OPEN TABLE

HOLY COMMUNION

Invitation

People will come from east and west, north and south—gay and straight, bisexual and transgendered; black, white, red, and brown; apparently healthy and physically, mentally, and emotionally challenged—and sit at table with our God. All are welcome to God's meal spread for us this day.

Eucharistic Prayer

Creator God, we give you thanks for making us—all of us—in your image and giving us life. We remember how you fed your wandering people in the desert with manna and sustained them on their journey to the promised land. We thank you for your coming into your creation as the blessed one, Jesus, feeding the throngs who followed you with bread and fish. We rejoice that you came as risen Christ to the dispirited disciples in the Upper Room, the Emmaus home, and the mount in Galilee. We praise you for your Holy Spirit, who continues to feed, guide, and instruct us this day and every day. By your power keep your people steadfast in telling your good news in all the world. Turn us with hope to Christ's triumphant welcome, which will gather us at the great heavenly feast. With all God's people, united through Christ's love and by the Holy Spirit's power, we rejoice in your righteous love that renews all to your honor and glory, now and forever. Amen.

—*Rev. Judith Ann Becker*

COMMUNION RESOURCES

Call to Worship for a Communion Service

ONE: Humans have been successful at building walls in the name of religion.

*ALL:We are good at finding names to brand others unfit
to be with us in our fellowship.*

ONE: But just when we think we know who is to be included,

ALL: God has a way of breaking through and inviting them in.

ONE: And so foreigners, strangers, eunuchs, outcasts,
all have found their place at the table of our God.

*ALL: So the table has come to include male and female,
but also intersexed, omnigendered children of the Creator.*

ONE: Today let us all celebrate, for all are welcome says our God.

Invitation

ONE: Gather us in, O God, from all our journeys.

ALL: Gather us in—the lost and forsaken, the proud and the strong.

ONE: Gather us—the gay and the straight, the intersexed as well as the male and female.

ALL: Gather us in to this place where Good News is shared.

ONE: Gather us in to the table that God sets before us all.

ALL: Gather us in by your Spirit, O God, that we may be one together.

Prayer for the Great Thanksgiving

ONE: God be with you.

ALL: And also with you.

ONE: Lift up your hearts.

ALL:We lift them up to God.

ONE: Let us give thanks to God Most High.

ALL: It is right to give God thanks and praise.

ONE: It is right and good, always and everywhere to give thanks to you,
God Almighty, Creator of heaven and earth.
In the beginning you created us in your image as human beings
needing relationship with other human beings.
You have shared your grace and love
through the others who enter our lives.
When we cause others pain, you give forgiveness.
When others cause us pain, you bring comfort.
In the life of Jesus of Nazareth you reveal new understandings
of love that break down the dividing walls of judgment.
In particular we recall your grace and your Spirit
poured out on people of all sexual and gender identities,
on people turned away from families and jobs
when they come out of the closet,
on individuals told how terrible they are
when they have simply sought to live
as the persons they believe God has made them to be.
With these, with all of your people,
and with the company of heaven, we glorify you:

ALL: Holy, holy, holy God of love and majesty,
the whole universe speaks of your glory,
O God most high.
Blessed is the One who comes in the name of our God!
Hosanna in the Highest!

ONE: Holy are you, God, and blessed is your child Jesus.
We remember how Jesus came to share your love,
to reach out to the stranger, to these condemned by society,
to the sick and sorrowing, to the unloved and the persecuted.
In particular we remember how on the night of betrayal
Jesus took and broke the bread, gave you thanks,
shared it with the disciples,
inviting them, and now us, to eat of the broken body
that suffered indignation and pain
for all God's children, and to do so in remembrance.
Likewise Jesus took the cup, gave you thanks, shared it with the disciples,

inviting them, and now us, to drink of this blood of the new covenant
for all God's children, and to do so in remembrance.
As we share this table, we boldly speak of our belief:

ALL: Christ has died, Christ is risen, Christ will come again.

ONE: Now gracious God, we invite your Holy Spirit
to bless this bread and cup
that they may be for us the body and blood of Christ
our Sovereign and our Savior.
Make us the body of Christ as Church, welcoming all who come,
gay and straight, transsexual, male and female,
stranger at our gates and close friend,
as you have welcomed us in loving relationship.
In the name of the Christ.

ALL: Amen.

—*Rev. David Schmidt*

Another Prayer for the Great Thanksgiving

ONE: God be with you.

ALL: And also with you.

ONE: Lift up your hearts.

ALL: We lift them up to God.

ONE: Let us give thanks to God Most High.

ALL: It is right to give God thanks and praise.

ONE: It is right and good, always and everywhere to give thanks to you.
God Almighty, Creator of heaven and earth and of all who dwell therein:
God of the first children, God of Abraham and Sarah and Hagar,
God of Moses and Miriam, God of Mary and Joseph,
God of our forebears who shared your story through the ages,
God of our mothers and our fathers, our sisters and our brothers,
God of male and female, of transgendered and omnigendered,
God of gays and lesbians, of bisexuals and heterosexuals.
In your grace and love you have called all of us to your side.
You have poured out your Spirit upon us all,
and you have called us to your table of sacrifice and love.
And so, with your people now on earth

and with the company of the saints,
we praise your name and join them in singing:

ALL: Holy, holy, holy God of love and majesty,
the whole universe speaks of your glory,
O God Most High.
Blessed is the One who comes in the name of our God!
Hosanna in the highest!

ONE: Holy are you, God, and blessed is your child Jesus.
We remember how Jesus came to share your love,
to reach out to the stranger, to these condemned by society,
to the sick and sorrowing, to the unloved and the persecuted.
In particular we remember how on the night of betrayal
Jesus took and broke the bread, gave you thanks,
shared it with the disciples,
inviting them, and now us, to eat of the broken body
that suffered indignation and pain
for all God's children, and to do so in remembrance.
Likewise Jesus took the cup, gave you thanks, shared it with the disciples,
inviting them, and now us, to drink of this blood of the new covenant
for all God's children, and to do so in remembrance.
As we share this table, we boldly speak of our belief:

ALL: Christ has died, Christ is risen, Christ will come again.

ONE: Now, gracious God, we invite your Holy Spirit
to bless this bread and cup
that they may be for us the body and blood of Christ
our Sovereign and our Savior.
Make us the body of Christ as Church, welcoming all who come,
gay and straight, transsexual, male and female,
stranger at our gates and close friend,
as you have welcomed us in loving relationship.
In the name of the Christ.

ALL: Amen.

—*Rev. David Schmidt*

(For a transgender informed interpretation of the Last Supper, see the
exegesis of the water carrier in Lewis Payne's story, chapter 19.)

28

MANY VOICES
RESPONSIVE READINGS, LITANIES, AND RITUALS

THE MARVEL OF HUMANKIND—A PRAYER

ONE: Radiant Source of Life,
you have created human beings alike yet diverse.
Birthed in your image,
we are thrust into light, into air, into possibility,
each of us a mystery ever unfolding.

*ALL: We find ourselves delighted;
we find ourselves confounded
by the marvel of humankind.*

ONE: Loving God,
forgive us when from days of breast or bottle,
we feed our children on stereotype and fear,
making them wary of themselves and others.
Move us to supplant ignorance with understanding
and indifference with care.

ALL: Forgive us when we wrap our children
in clothing or dreams that constrict
their uniqueness.
Fill us with love that guides and frees them,
body and spirit,
to be their truest selves.

ONE: Help us to honor the rich complexities of who we are,
remembering that you, O God, have made humanness
more than just "this" or "that."
More than only black or white,

ALL: we are an array of skin tones and concepts of color.

ONE: More than the split of pink or blue,

ALL: we are evergreen, amethyst, and silver in gender.

ONE: More than a divide of homosexual or heterosexual,

ALL: we are a variable spectrum of loves and attractions.

ONE: More than plainly disabled or able,

ALL: we are a range of capabilities and talents.

ONE: Source of our being and of all blessing,
deepen and unite us in you,
so that we may know ourselves and others to be

ALL: bearers of your creative power,
witnesses to your transforming love,
and channels of your sustaining grace.

ONE AND ALL: Amen.

Rev. Ann D. Day

CREDO

I believe that there is only one God.
I believe that God is devoid of all ego.
I believe that God is composed of many attributes,
such as love, compassion, forgiveness, faithfulness, and more.
I believe that God is a god of many names and answers to them all.
I believe that no one book could contain all there is to know
about God or God's path.
I believe that there are many holy scriptures

to edify, build, empower, and change lives
   so that they can become more like God.
I believe God to be all inclusive.
I believe that everything was created by God.
I believe that God is within all things.
I believe that God is the life force.
I believe that God is the sustainer of all life.
I believe that we are all one with God, earth, nature, and all creation.
I believe that all life is sacred. Do no harm.
I believe that God is omnigendered.
I believe that all people were created in God's image
   and are aspects of that image.
I believe we all have the right to rituals and sacraments
   that will enhance our lives and expressions of God.
I believe in the importance of congregational worship and fellowship.

I believe that Jesus Christ was the incarnation of God
   and an example of the incarnated God in each individual.
I believe that Jesus Christ was the divine example of inclusiveness.
I believe that Jesus Christ was the divine example of unconditional love.
I believe that Jesus Christ's purpose was to teach us a way of life:
   to show us that faith lies between the individual and God,
   to remove the corruptible intermediary of institutionalized religion.

—*Ashley Moore*

PRAYER FOR DELIVERANCE

O God, deliver us.
From the anger we turn inward, or misdirect toward those we love,
deliver us.
From wanting our opponents' downfall rather than their liberation,
deliver us.
From fear, anxiety, stress, or loneliness that makes us seek a quick fix of
religious or political absolutes, of drugs or alcohol, of compulsive sexual
expressions or messianic lover,
O God, deliver us.
From believing what "they" say about us, devaluing ourselves
or others like us,
deliver us.

From isolation from sisters and brothers, and ghettoization
of our existence,
deliver us.
From lack of trust and faith in ourselves as individuals
and ourselves as community,
O God deliver us.
From denial of our integrity as spiritual-sexual creations,
deliver us.
From rejection of others because of their body-state, whether gender,
race, age, sexual orientation, appearance, or disability,
*O God deliver us. Free us to live your commonwealth, O God. Clarify our vision,
purify our motives, renew our hope. In the name of you who creates us, of the Christ
who calls us, and of the Spirit who empowers us, Amen.*

—*Chris R. Glaser, from* Coming Out to God, *John Knox Press,1990.
   Used by permission of the author.*

LEAVING HOME/COMING HOME/CREATING FAMILY

LEADER: We are God's people!

*PEOPLE: God's good people—lesbian, gay, bisexual, transgender,
and those who stand in solidarity with us.*

LEADER: We are God's people!

*PEOPLE: God's beautiful people—brown as the earth; pale as moonlight; black as
the night; red as the sunset; golden as sunlight—we are God's living rainbow.*

LEADER: We are God's people!

*PEOPLE: Dancing God's seasons—
children who skip to a wordless tune;
young people who move to new rhythms each day;
adults who march and wheel to the steady beat
of a distinctly different drummer;
and those elders who've danced all the dances
and now step securely in well-chosen waltz-time.*

LEADER: We are God's people!

*PEOPLE: A family like no other—and all like family to each other.
We leave home to come home to create family.*

LEADER: We are God's people and yet we found "home" to be a place of exodus—a wilderness place where we cannot rest.

PEOPLE: *Because "home" was anger, abandonment, abuse, and denial;*
"home" was closeted, painful, and oppressive;
"home" was unhealthy, uncomfortable, unloving, and unkind;
"home" was rejection, guilt, damage, and brokenness.

LEADER: And this wilderness home, this place of anguish, is a place that we should only pass through on the road to the new "home"— the "home" just barely visible and still being imagined by spirited souls full of possibility.

PEOPLE: *We taste the new home at table fellowship*
with our spiritual sisters and brothers,
who in our religious communities become the family
we cry with, call out to, laugh with, hug, hold
and celebrate with on our special days.

LEADER: We need that new home with friends who know our stories, parents who move beyond rejection, partners who share our dreams.

PEOPLE: *We hear that new home in the laughter of children:*
our daughters and sons, nieces and nephews,
sisters and brothers, cousins and grandchildren.

LEADER: We feel that new home in the quiet presence we bring to those suffering with AIDS, their partners, families, and friends— sharing what we have: our time, our talent, our prayers.

PEOPLE: *We vision our new home in the breaking down of the old*
and the building up of the new—
our new home is furnished with our stories, role models and martyrs,
heroines and heroes, parades and protests, rituals and affirmations,
blessings and family reunions.

LEADER: We are your people, O God!

PEOPLE: *We are your people, O God!*
And when we come home to you, you know us as your people.
Amen and amen.

—*Mid-Atlantic Affirmation, written for the 1988 interfaith Gay and Lesbian Pride Service. Published in* Open Hands *(Winter 1990). Used by permission.*

WHO IS ME?

Who is Me?

Am I the suited leader on the Board of Trustees, representing the church, leading worship, respected and unknown, counted on as sure as the shaven face they think they see?

Who is Me?

Am I the dad in dungarees, sweats and sneaks, raking leaves with my boys, assigning curfews and giving baritone lectures on the mystery of dating girls?

Who is Me?

Am I the plaid cotton shirt with khakis comfortably admitted into places of business with my sage and simple black attaché case that holds so many questions?

Who is Me?

Am I the padded and pajama'd one who shuts off the TV and heads to the bedroom to lay a tired head on my pillow, ending a satisfying day of labor, luxury, and laundry?

Who is Me?

Am I the lady, painted and plucked, buxom and bawdy, sexy and silly, prancing and dancing, as the bedroom door closes and my hips saunter to the trembling treble within?

Dear and Holy God,
Me is ALL.
I know you know.
My secrets are heavy and sweet.

I weave all of me from threads of You,
I am fearfully and wonderfully made, so colorfully and diversely cloaked.
Soon, the bedroom door will be opened and I will be revealed.

Thanks. Amen.

— *Pastor Judith Hanlon, from interviews with transgendered parishioners, still closeted. Hearing their words from the pulpit she is convinced that authentic celebration is beginning.*

AN AFFIRMATION OF FAITH

As children of God, we celebrate the beauty and individual worth
of all creation.
We believe in God:

who created each of us, who breathed into us our uniqueness,
who delights in who we are, and what we can still become.

We believe in the love of God:

who laughs with us in our joy, who cries with us in our pain,
who wants all creation to seek peace, reconciliation, and love for each other.

We believe in the justice of God as revealed in scripture, and
through the lives of prophets of yesterday and today.

God alone created us. We are not alone; God loves us.
Nothing will separate us from the love of God.

—*Reconciling Congregation Program, Third National Convocation, 1993,*
    from Shaping Sanctuary: Proclaiming God's Grace in an Inclusive Church,
    ed. Kelly Turney, 2000. Used by permission.

CONFESSION AND ASSURANCE OF GRACE

ONE: In the very act of praising God, we become most aware of our
separations, from one another and from God. Even together, we stand alone,
and alone, together we search our hearts. Let us pray:

ALL: Our Mother, Father God,
We are accepting people, but many of our churches still bear "do not enter" signs,
    and we have not challenged them as we might.
We hear many congregations claiming to be open, but there are people who are
    still kept from their tables, and our protests, if any, have been too soft.
Forgive us, God, and make us the strong, inclusive people we are called to be.
In a world that divides itself by culture, class, color, and appearance, we strive to
    be the voice of tolerance.
Yet we sometimes tolerate the intolerance of others out of our own insecurity of
    fearing what we do not understand.
We allow the insulation of our privilege to protect us because we do not know
    how to reach the disenfranchised people of our world.
We are uneasy dealing with those who enter our well-vacuumed worlds bearing
    the stench of hard life.

We do not know how to get them to our tables, and we fear what might happen if we did.

We also withdraw from those who reject our acceptance of others.

How hard it is to love those who hate, and how hard to include them at our tables as well.

Forgive us, God, and make us the strong, inclusive people we are called to be. Amen.

ONE: We belong to a God of love and compassion. We believe that God can make all things new. So I say to you, in the name of Jesus the Christ, who empowers us all, we are forgiven.

ALL: Thanks be to God for forgiveness.

Thanks be to God for love, and for calling us forth, ever strong, ever open to new life.

—*Reconciling Congregation Program, Fifth National Convocation, 1997, from* Shaping Sanctuary: Proclaiming God's Grace in an Inclusive Church, *ed. Kelly Turney, 2000. Used by permission.*

"I AM"

A Liturgy of Re-Naming for Transgender Persons

Scripture: Revelation 21:1–6

ONE: Dearly beloved, as a people of faith, we know that God continues to shape and mold us in our growth, inviting us to claim for ourselves the people who God created us to be. Each new day is an opportunity to live more fully the promise of who we are.

Throughout history, individuals, as they have claimed their unique personhood more fully, have been given new names, a testimony of their faithfulness.

ALL: Abram was renamed Abraham.

ONE: Sarai was renamed Sarah.

ALL: Simon was renamed Peter.

ONE: Saul was renamed Paul.

ALL: We know that renaming is an important way to reflect our new nature found in Christ.

One: Today a child of God comes forward in an important renaming. It has not been an easy journey, yet we know that the road of faith is not an easy one. We have been asked to witness this renaming and become companions for the journey.

My friend, throughout your life you have been known as _____ (former name). The Holy Spirit, however, continued to call forth within you something more. Today, you stand before us, your life a testimony to the God who makes all things new. What name do you choose for yourself?

Person being renamed: I am _____ (new name).

One: You have known the waters of baptism, when you were claimed as God's own. Today we again use water, as a reminder to you that God continues to claim you and sustain you. May these waters refresh and renew you in your journey of faith.

([New name] cups hands over a basin while water is poured from a pitcher. He/She draws this water to his/her lips.)

One: _____ (new name), you are God's beloved child. May you continue to be a faithful follower of Jesus, glorifying God through all that you do and all that you are.

My friends, I present to you _____ (new name).

All: _____ (new name), we rejoice with you for all that God has done for you, and for all that has yet to be revealed. As your sisters and brothers, we pledge to walk with you, as you will walk with us. Together we shall drink water from the well of life. May the life and ministry we share always reflect that love of God, which calls us all to wholeness.

—*Rev. Karen Oliveto, reprinted with permission of the author, from* Open Hands *(Fall 1996) and* Shaping Sanctuary: Proclaiming God's Grace in an Inclusive Church, *ed. Kelly Turney, 2000.*

A SERVICE OF SPIRITUAL BAPTISM

Invitation

Officiant: In the beginning God was lonely. Out of that great heart of divine love we were created in God's image. Let us praise our Creator in song. (Sing an appropriate hymn.)

Statement of Purpose

We are called as followers of Jesus Christ and children of God, the Author, Sustainer and Redeemer of all life, to be a community of witness for the spiritual baptism of _____ and in so doing to accept, reaffirm, and rededicate this child of God.

Statement of Faith

We enter this world as tiny babies, children of the Creator of all life. Some of us are born wholly male and some, wholly female. Some of us are born fractured, broken in a way we are not able to discern at first. Still all of us are born in God's image.

It is God who creates, sustains, renews, redeems, and gives purpose to our lives. It is God who has given to each of us the image of the Divine that we bear spiritually. Created by love, we are called to live in love with each person here and in intimate love with our Creator.

In Jesus of Nazareth, we have seen God, even if through a glass darkly. We have learned of our heavenly Parent's great love for us. We learn from Jesus' teachings, his example, his life, his death, and his resurrection that God wills for us only that which is good, pure, born of love.

The Holy Spirit filled Christ, resting upon him like a dove from the time of his baptism by John and throughout his ministry. The Holy Spirit is the manifestation of God's divine personality in the midst of humanity and the world, the very being of God set loose in life.

It is in this way that God works in our lives, leads us to the fulfillment of our purpose, guides and sustains us in love. In accepting the Holy Spirit into our lives we proclaim our love of God and enter into oneness with God.

Prayer for the Gift of the Holy Spirit

OFFICIANT: Let us pray.

ALL: O God, this child, born of your hand and divine love, _____, born broken, torn between two human natures, through your divine grace has been set free, made whole, renewed, and now comes to you, O Almighty One, and before your family (wholly male/wholly female) seeking the baptism of your Holy Spirit. For this we give thanks to you.

(S/he) who has been baptized by water and word in the name of the Trinity into the community of Christ during (his/her) brokenness comes now before you to be baptized _____ in you and by your Holy Spirit, and to be reaffirmed and renewed in the acceptance of this community of faith. (S/he) comes here to rededicate (her/him) self to your divine will as revealed to us by Christ Jesus. We

all give thanks and praise to you, O Holy One, for the wholeness you have bestowed upon (him / her) by your great love. Amen.

Individual Commitment

OFFICIANT: Do you, _____ , promise to give all of yourself anew to the life of love as commanded of us by God through Jesus Christ in the Holy Spirit?

SEEKER: With the help of Almighty God, I do so pledge my life to God and the community of faith to live according to the commandment of love in this world and the next.

Blessing

OFFICIANT (placing both hands on the seeker's head): As God's minister of the good news of divine love proclaimed by Christ I baptize you _____ in the name of the Creator, Jesus the Christ, and the Holy Spirit. (Placing baptismal stole yoked over seeker) Hence forth on earth and through-out eternity before mortal and divine you shall be known as _____.

Congregational Commitment

Do you as children of God and brothers and sisters accept this once frac-tured child as a whole (sister/brother) and promise to walk beside (him/her) and sustain this (brother/sister) in (his/her) journey and the service of Christ Jesus, Almighty God and the Holy Spirit?

ALL: As children of God, God being our Great Helper, and as sisters and brothers of Jesus, the Blessed One, we do rejoice in this healing, growth, and rededication of our (sister/brother) to the life of love. We rededicate our lives also to the divine com-mandment of love and promise to sustain (her/him) and walk with (him//her) as Christ walked in the service of God, the Almighty Lover of us all.

Concluding Hymn and Benediction

—Rev. Joanna Louise

BLESSING A NEW NAME

(Small Ceremony in a Congregation)

LEADER: Hear the words of scripture from the book of Revelation: "Let anyone who has an ear listen to what the Spirit is saying to the churches. To everyone who conquers I will give some of the hidden manna, and I will give a white stone, and on the white stone is written a new name that no one knows except the one who receives it." (Rev. 2:17)

God changed the name of Sarai to Sarah and Jacob to Israel to describe their blessing, God changed the names of Gomer and Hosea's children from Lo-Ruhamah to Ruhamah—Not Pitied to Pitied, from Lo-Ammi to Ammi—Not My People to My People, to reconcile and bring hope. God recognized that Simon would also always be called Peter and Dorcas called Tabitha, because some people will always be known by more than one name.

And when Moses asked God, "Who should I say sent me?" God answered, "I Am Who I Am"(Gen. 17:15; Gen. 32:28; Hos. 1:8–9, 2:1; Matt. 16:17–18; Acts 9:36; Ex. 3:14).

(The leader hands a single white stone to the person who has a new name for blessing.)

Today we celebrate a new naming. Our brother/sister was known as _____ (any names, nicknames, titles, all the names that have been used in the past). Now he/she has received a new name, which is a gift from God, and has brought that gift to be shared in this congregation.

What new name have you received?

NEWLY NAMED: My name is _____. "I Am" has called me _____.

CONGREGATION: God, we give you thanks for ——————— *and for his/her ability to claim that name—accepting the blessings, acknowledging the difficult journey, and anticipating the ambiguities of being known in different ways by different people. We thank you for your great "I Am," which makes possible our "I am," and we pray through the matchless name of Jesus. Amen.*

LEADER: With us today are people who are very special to _____. You have been a part of his/her journey. Please come forward to greet and bless this child of God.

(Some come forward, perhaps family members, friends, a therapist or doctor. The person whose name is being blessed should have a small basket with white stones with his/her name printed on them. As each person comes forward he or she will receive a stone and place a hand on the head of the one being named in a blessing gesture or shake hands, saying: "I greet you, _____, and I bless you. Amen.

After all but the person being named have returned to their seats, the congregation offers the following blessing:)

CONGREGATION: *In the name of God, "I Am Who I Am," we greet you, _____, and we bless you. Wherever you go, know that I Am has sent you. Amen.*

(All may be seated.)

—*Maren C. Tirabassi*

CEREMONY FOR FAMILY ACCEPTANCE AND RECONCILIATION

Small Ceremony in a Congregation

(For this celebration the transperson comes forward in the congregation with three people prepared to offer blessings. One should be a member of an older generation in the family—a parent, grandparent, uncle, or aunt, or a person chronologically older who can stand on this occasion as a godparent. The second should be a member of the same generation—brother, sister, cousin, or dear friend—and the third a younger person—a child, niece, nephew, or the child of a friend. Included is also a blessing for a former or current spouse. As each speaks, using the words of this ceremony or his or her own words, members of that generation may rise. At the conclusion of each statement a gift is given. Appropriate would be clothing for the chosen gender such as a scarf or a tie.

A visual presentation may be the wearing of a stole quilted from fabric at one end that remembers the gender of the past and continuing to the new gender. During the reception a similar effect can be created by a rainbow-shaped collage of photographs from childhood to the present.)

LEADER: Listen to the words of scripture.

(Choose one or more of these texts.)

"So if anyone is in Christ, there is a new creation: everything old has passed away; see, everything has become new!" (2 Cor. 5:17).

"But the father said to his slaves, 'Quickly, bring out a robe—the best one—and put it on him; put a ring on his finger and sandals on his feet. And get the fatted calf and kill it, and let us eat and celebrate; for this son of mine was dead and is alive again; he was lost and is found!' And they began to celebrate" (Luke 15:22–24).

"Do not remember the former things, or consider the things of old. I am about to do a new thing; now it springs forth, do you not perceive it? I will make a way in the wilderness and rivers in the desert. The wild animals will honor me, the jackals and the ostriches; for I give water in the wilderness and rivers in the desert, to give drink to my chosen people, the people whom I formed for myself so that they might declare my praise" (Isa. 43:18–21).

"Now Jacob looked up and saw Esau coming and four hundred men with him. . . . He himself went on ahead of them, bowing himself to the ground seven times, until he came near his brother. But Esau ran to meet him, and embraced him, and fell on his neck and kissed him, and they wept" (Gen. 33:1, 3, 4).

"So when you are offering your gift at the altar, if you remember that your brother or sister has something against you, leave your gift there before the altar and go; first be reconciled to your brother or sister, and then come and offer your gift" (Matt. 5:23–24).

"So then you are no longer strangers and aliens, but you are citizens with the saints and also members of the household of God, built upon the foundation of the apostles and prophets, with Christ Jesus himself as the cornerstone. In him the whole structure is joined together and grows into a holy temple in the Lord; in whom you also are built together spiritually into a dwelling place for God" (Eph. 2:19–22).

MEMBER OF THE OLDER GENERATION: _____, receive the blessing of those who have known you for many years. We give thanks for memories of your childhood and youth, even though we know that many times were difficult. We ask your forgiveness for all those times we failed to understand you fully. We respectfully ask to become a part of your new life and celebrate your presence in our family.

(Giving of gift)

MEMBER OF THE SAME GENERATION: _____, receive the blessing of those who have known you as both male and female. We have not always understood your intense need for transition but we have always loved you. Help us to grow with you and celebrate your presence in our family.

(Giving of gift)

MEMBER OF THE YOUNGER GENERATION: _____, receive the blessing of those who look up to you and learn about courage, honesty, and integrity from your decision. Our possibilities are broadened by celebrating your presence in our family.

(Giving of gift)

Spouse/former spouse: _____, I have loved you and my life has changed because of your decisions. Help me to support all of your transition even as I honestly ask you to reach out and respond to the deepest needs in my life. I celebrate your presence in the midst of our/your family.

(Giving of gift)

(Other significant members and friends may wish to speak.)

Transgender person leading in prayer: Gracious God, I give you thanks not only for your blessing of me in this transition in my life, but also for the way I have been surrounded by family. I recognize that some were shaken and disturbed by a reality so obvious to me that sometimes I forgot to help them understand. I am so glad that these good people are still with me today. (May wish to include the following: "Others have not chosen to be a part of my new life and I grieve their absence. I let them go with hope, knowing that you use experiences to change and help people into new understandings. I release bitterness inside me, which would be toxic to my life and this family.") Bless these dear people, and teach me to be present for them—as they have been present for me—in all the changes of life. I pray through the Holy Spirit who makes family of us all. Amen.

Leader (laying on a hand of blessing or shaking hands, whichever is more comfortable): May the grace found in this moment of acceptance, reconciliation, and celebration continue to grow for _____, who is a child of God, and this family, which is a household of faith. May each one who gathers here today be blessed by the full realization of themselves, the care and nurture of loving human arms, and the assurance of God's embrace. Amen.

—*Maren C. Tirabassi*

29

HYMN LYRICS

Because You Love Me

I reach out to find the light from a star
A light so bright yet from afar
A light that defines infinite beauty
An inkling of truth, a sense of duty.

The wisdom of truth encourages change
Becoming a struggle to gently arrange
The tender strands of life meant to be
Sleeping no longer, learning to see.

Dreams and visions help courage appear
The image is daunting, a birth is near
Gently one searches to find the parts
That go together to fill our hearts.

A journey within, fills us with feelings
Presenting a newness, with many glass ceilings
Like layers and layers of stars in the sky
One learns to look beyond the white lie.

A virgin vision is fixed in the mind
Newly defined as one of a kind
The child is born to grow and abide
A new existence that can't be denied.

The universe takes on its role to nourish
The child grows and begins to flourish
Despite the closeness the family portrays
Their haste to reject defines their ways.

Time tells its story, lives grow and begin
A family answers a cry from within.
Their love to nurture, to care and embrace
Works its magic, with loving grace.

Finding the essence of God's creation
Her heart often fills with grateful elation
Because you loved her, she knows that she is
Loved just because she just is

Refrain: Because you love me I stand up tall
Because you love me I have it all
Because you love me I can go on
Becoming whole because I belong.

—Dzintra Alksnitis

The following lyrics may be used alone or added to a traditional singing
of the hymn. The music is, in all cases, in the public domain.

Just As I Am

Just as I am, your holy child,
My truth so fragile, undefiled.
I turned to you and then you smiled—
O Lamb of God, I come, I come.

Just as I am though others curse,
and label me—profane, perverse.
Now all your love, my universe,
O Lamb of God, I come, I come.

—Maren C. Tirabassi

Jesus Calls Us, O'er the Tumult

Jesus calls us when the tumult
comes from deep within our breast.
Man or woman, newfound gender,
feel acceptance, love, and rest.

"Born again?" asked Nicodemus.
How can we return that way?
With our God all things are promised.
Trust the Spirit and obey.

—M. C. T.

Breathe on Me, Breath of God

Breathe on me, Breath of God,
and make my gender true.
Return my earthly shape again,
to that which pleases you.

Breathe on me, Breath of God,
teach me to trust my heart,
a woman's song or man's bright eye,
true to your matchless art.

—M. C. T.

Amazing Grace

Amazing grace, expressed in change—
in voice in shape, in stance.
As butterfly from chrysalis,
My spirit starts to dance.

So many years the questions churned—
my life within, without.
But now my body has returned,
and hope replaces doubt.

—M. C. T.

For the Beauty of the Earth

For the joy of human form
shaped to meet the inner soul.
Man or woman, each reborn,
flowering out, becoming whole—
God of all to you we raise
this our hymn of grateful praise.

For transgendered rainbow sign,
after floods of human tears,
arks of safety in the past,
claiming faith and conquering fears—
God of all to you we raise
this our hymn of grateful praise.

For the church with open doors,
for the pews where all can rest,
for each child by love restored,
for the man and woman blessed—
God of all to you we raise
this our hymn of grateful praise.

—M. C. T.

30

A CHILDREN'S STORY
WINDSONG

"WHAT YOU sow does not come to life unless it dies. And what you sow is not the body which is to be, but a bare kernel, perhaps of wheat or of some other grain. But God gives it a body as he has chosen, and to each kind of seed its own body" (1 Cor. 15:36(b)–38 RSV).

The Wind blew a seed, along with many others, up into the air.

Frightened, the little seed cried, "Where am I going? What will happen to me?"

"You are going to a new place," replied the Wind. "When you get there, you will sleep through the winter and change in the spring."

"Change?"

"You must let what is inside you come out," the wind whispered. "You will put down roots, send up a green shoot, and grow leaves. You won't be a seed any more."

"But I know how to be a seed! I'm afraid to change. If I'm not a seed anymore, I won't be me. I'll have died."

"Nothing comes to life unless it dies," said a little, yellow leaf who was falling down from a nearby tree, rushing to the ground below.

"You can't die until you live," added a dust mote, dancing in the air.

"You can't live until you love," said a small spider who floated past, attached to a little sail she had made from her silk.

Suddenly the tiny seed landed—plop!—in some good dirt next to a garden fence.

A squirrel, looking for nuts, stepped on the seed and pushed it into the ground. Helpful earthworms, looking for leaves to eat, carried it deep beneath the ground.

"So," complained the seed, "what if I don't change?"

"Look around you," the worms told the seed. "Some of this dirt was made from seeds who never changed. If something tries to live without changing, it will die."

"How can a seed live if it isn't a seed anymore? I don't understand."

"Dig in the earth after a seed grows, and you find only the new plant the seed becomes. Seeds are God's promises that haven't happened yet."

The tiny seed decided to have courage. After winter's long sleep, it sent out roots, green shoots, and leaves.

"Look, Wind," cried the new plant, "I'm a girl! I thought I was, but I never knew till I let what was inside me come out. "

She grew and grew, quickly sending out long green arms with special leaves that could wind and grip other things to lift her up and along the fence, closer to the sun.

"I'm a very long woman," she giggled to the Wind.

"You are becoming a vine of some sort. Keep changing."

She spread green leaves and long arms over much of the fence. She made buds and grew beautiful white flowers shaped like trumpets with lovely pink stripes at their center.

"What a pretty morning glory," said the boy who worked every day in the garden. "I think that's my favorite flower."

"I'm a Morning Glory," she laughed. She was very happy.

Little pods holding baby seeds appeared along her length. She told the Wind about it: "I've made seeds! But now that I've finished that promise, I'm afraid again. When I was a seed, I changed and became a plant. But what now? I'm already a plant. There is nothing left to become except a dry husk turning into dirt."

"And, what is wrong with dirt?" grumbled the Earth beneath her.

Surprised, she quickly apologized, "I'm sorry. Nothing is wrong with dirt. Earth has always been there for me and I couldn't live without you. It could be another answered promise of God's for me to join you."

"I understand, dear," replied the Earth. "And a part of you will join me. But surely you don't think God made only one or two promises when Divine Breath gave you life?"

Soon, the frost came. Glory lifted her bursting pods to the Wind and sent her seeds into its breath. Her vines and leaves wilted. Her dry body fell to the ground.

As she saw all this happen to her, Glory suddenly shouted in wonder: "Hey, how am I seeing this? Who am I? What am I?"

She blew up and about, lifting all the colored leaves in the garden, searching for an answer. She could fly! She laughed with joy and played tag with the tail of a little black kitten. Seeing the gardening boy come out, she blew an autumn kiss on his lips and put a red blush on his cheeks.

"Wind," she exclaimed. "I'm part of the Wind."

"Yes," the Breath of God laughed around her, "you are."

"How?"

"A brave and loving spirit is the breath of God," the Wind replied.

"You can't live till you change," she whispered.

"You don't change until you give," added a little brown leaf.

"You don't live unless you love," came the voice of the gardening boy, not aware he was talking to anyone but himself.

"Some words mean almost the same promise," came a voice on the Wind: "Love, life, wind, Jesus, breath, spirit, God."

Glory had to ask, "Where do I go now?"

"Everywhere God breathes," replied the Wind. "Come, Glory, I have many more promises to share." And, perhaps carrying a story, the Wind blew along.

—*Rev. Sheryl Stewart*

31

BIBLE STUDIES

EUNUCHS ARE WELCOME

Isaiah 56:1–8, Acts 8:26–40

MOST OFTEN CONVERSATIONS ABOUT HOMOSEXUALITY and the Bible deal with seven texts. Traditionally the Bible is understood to deal with two basic sexual identities—male and female. However, there is at least a third sexual identity—eunuchs. Reflection on their role in scripture may be informative to all of us.

Early biblical tradition does, indeed, primarily focus on male and female. The Genesis 1 creation narrative is an example. The Torah, in its concern for purity, outlaws eunuchs from Temple worship (Deut. 23). But eunuchs continually show up. The word occurs twenty-nine times, according to my count. Many times these are court people. Only in Deuteronomy and Leviticus are they negative portrayals. As several have suggested, this third sex may be closest to gay-les-bi-trans.

In Isaiah 56, eunuchs and foreigners (contra Torah) are proclaimed welcome kin. Antigay writers frequently take issue with their inability to

have children, as if that were essential for God's love. The text in Isaiah re-
veals that God values a faithful response more than progeny. The "kin-dom"
of God, as envisioned by the time of the great prophets, contains more
than those the Torah and its early rules for cleanliness foresaw.

In Matthew 19, Jesus also offers an interesting aside. He describes
three kinds of eunuchs—those born so (presumably, transsexuals), those
made so by others, and those choosing chastity. Jesus never speaks about
homosexuality, but this text witnesses to his compassion for those with
gender deviation from the religious norms. From Jesus' teaching of love
for all, Paul concludes in Galations 3 that there is in Christ no longer male
and female. In the kin-dom, or realm of God, distinctions do not arise
from sexual identity!

Finally, in Acts 8 we meet the Ethiopian eunuch. In two ways his religious status is in doubt. By remembering and telling the conversion of a
mysterious black from Timbuktu, a God-fearer, presumably prevented
from entering the Temple because of the stipulations of Deuteronomy, the
writer of Acts demonstrates for the first and a dramatic time God's grace
and Spirit moving beyond the boundaries of Judaism. The early Christians
must respond to the eunuch's reception of the Holy Spirit at his baptism.
Prior to baptism, his status may have been in doubt. After his baptism, it
cannot be.

And so, from these passages we reach a conclusion that eunuchs may
well be the ones to point the way. Certainly they may be transsexual, but
these passages speak to gay-les-bi as well. God's grace spills out where it
will. If God does not withhold the Spirit, how can we? The biblical experience shows the Spirit broadening the table to include eunuchs. Hence
here at Shalom Church we can proclaim with confidence, eunuchs are
welcome. The table of our God is spread, and all sexual and gender identities are welcome.

—Rev. David Schmidt

INTRODUCTION TO BIBLE STUDIES

The series of ten Bible studies that follow each consist of a text and five
questions. They are chosen to highlight issues facing transgender members of congregations or congregations learning to reach out to transgender people. However, each session asks questions inviting all participants
to share personally as well as "discuss issues." For example, in studying

Psalm 139 everyone is asked: "Have you ever tried to run away from God?" These study experiences should foster heart-connections as well as head-connections.

Appropriate would be some form of introductory ice-breaker, a leader's opening prayer or hymn, and a closing circle of prayer or mutual passing of the peace.

A Year of Cosmetics

Read Esther 2:7–18.

1. Have you ever spent a year (or a significant portion of time) in a primarily physical preparation, such as pregnancy, chemotherapy, weight watching, marathon training? How did that physical preparation influence your mind or impact your emotions?

2. Do you know what is involved as a physical commitment to gender reassignment?

3. Esther made many choices—to participate in the cosmetic preparations, to withhold information (such as her ancestry) to stay involved with her closest early relationship, to respect the advice of the court professional. How do some of these choices reflect issues that transgendered people face?

4. When Esther herself was chosen, or finished her transition to queen, there was an "Esther's banquet" and a holiday. How can a community create an "Esther's banquet" for a person in gender transition?

5. As the story of the book of Esther continues, it is clear that Esther will be in danger from others in the king's court if her background is revealed. What dangers do transgendered folks face when their background is exposed? How do you feel about the fact that she hid her background until disclosure was necessary for saving her people?

Cutting to the Bone

Read Ezekiel 37:1–14.

1. The vision of the valley of dry bones is about profound alienation. What situations in your life have made you feel disconnected, dried up, even lifeless?

2. Consider the situation of a person whose mind and body express different gender identities. In what ways would that experience compare to Ezekiel's description of skeletal remains?

3. This scripture is about a two-part resuscitation—first bones connecting and then spirit breathing. How do transgendered folks experience transition "body first, spirit second?"

4. In this scripture consider the relationship between God and the prophet. What are the distinct roles for each one of them?

5. Now put the local church in Ezekiel's role. How can the local church and God respond to folks who experience life as a valley of dry bones?

Riverdance and Reconciliation

Read Genesis 32:3–21 (especially 20 as background) and 22–32.

1. Family reconciliation can be very difficult and Jacob and Esau's reconciliation is one of the Bible's worst. Reflect on the background of their hostility. Then read about Jacob's preparation to meet Esau and his hope to be "accepted . . . when he sees my face."
   Why would the reentry of a transgendered person to a family be similarly complex?

2. Read verses 22–23. What kinds of wrestling with self and God are involved in changing gender identity?

3. The one who wrestles with Jacob has been variously identified as a demon, a "man," an angel, or God. How are all of these possible struggles for a transgendered person?

4. Jacob was renamed Israel. What is important to a transgendered person about change in a name? How does a family feel about a person changing his or her name?

5. Israel left the ford of the Jabbock limping and he limped for the rest of his life. What are the losses of transition?

A Couple Looks at Creation

Read Genesis 1:26–31 and Genesis 2:4b–7, 18–25.

1. These two stories of the sexual differentiation of humankind come from very different versions of creation narrative. Note the word "and" in 1:27 and the distinction between "adam" (human or man)

who is formed from the "adamah" (ground) in 2:7 and the new genders of "ish" (man) and "issah" (woman) in 2:23.

How are the two genders distinct? How are they connected? How is creation better for their uniqueness?

2. In chapter 2, what is wrong with the single human? What is God's plan to fix this? Can this plan be understood as surgical intervention in human unhappiness?

3. The removal of the rib and the presentation of the woman models division and return, change and reconciliation. Reflect on the process (including the deep sleep) as it relates to transgender issues.

4. How is making a gender transition an expression of creation?

5. In what ways do you need a partner, a helper . . . or to be a partner or helper?

When the Church Objects to Healing

Read Luke 13:10–17; Luke 14:1–6.

1. Reflect on the care with which Luke always used parallel parables, healing stories, and ethical examples that spotlight both men and women. Why does he do this? Does it matter to you?

2. What are your experiences with chronic ailments—physical, emotional, or spiritual?

3. Jesus heals the people with these chronic illnesses even though they could have lived for a long time so burdened and restricted. Discuss how Jesus would respond to a person who had experienced gender distress for a long time.

4. The religious authorities were angry about Jesus' healing because it broke their rules. What do you think of religious people who are critical of the human healing of gender change?

5. Given Jesus' response to the religious critique of his day, how do you think he responds now?

Tripping on the Armor

Read 1 Samuel 17, particularly verses 38–40.

1. The challenge of the Philistine giant Goliath was terrifying and overwhelming, but David decided to undertake it. What overwhelming tasks have you faced?

2. Saul thought he could protect David by putting him in the wrong clothes. Reflect on how transgendered folks can find "clothes"—aspects of appearance and behavior—as deeply wrong as unwieldy armor.

3. "I can't walk with these." Parents, jobs, church, society in general, insist on outfitting people. What practical ways can your church enable people to avoid awkward clothes. (Some possibilities might be eliminating gender-distinct clubs and groups, activities, and restrooms.)

4. How can we recognize and help people respond to appearance guidelines. How can we increase sensitivity?

5. What five things (your smooth stones for a slingshot) would you take into any difficult situation?

Stumbling Blocks and Stumps

Read Matthew 18:6–7 and 8–9.

1. Describe a personal situation of having a "stumbling block" put in front of you.

2. How do churches put stumbling blocks in the path of transgendered people developing a close relationship with God and a community of faith?

3. The second brief passage is one of Jesus' most enigmatic sayings. He seems to recommend surgical intervention! What do you think he meant?

4. What is a "transgender" interpretation of this passage?

5. Which is your greater danger—being hurt or denied access by someone else's stumbling block . . . or putting a stumbling block in the way of one of God's children?

VIPs

Read Matthew 19:10–12.

1. Use a concordance to study eunuchs in the biblical text. Look at the prohibitions and affirmations of eunuchs throughout scripture.

2. Jesus mentions three kinds of gender minorities. What are three gender minorities in contemporary society?

3. What are your experiences with gender minorities of any kind? Brainstorm a list from your group of all questions, doubts, fears, hopes, self-realizations. Acknowledge clearly that all questions are acceptable. Differentiate questions from opinions.

4. Where can your group go for answers to these questions—books, guests, videotapes? Take a look at the resource section in this book.

5. This passage appears between Jesus' criticism of hard-hearted divorce and Jesus' insistence (against the disciples' instincts) on blessing the children. What do we learn from this placement?

Fearfully, Wonderfully Made

Read Psalm 139.

1. Is the thought of God knowing you from before your birth comforting or disturbing? If God knows you that intimately, what is one thing that God knows about you?

2. Have you ever tried to run away from God?

3. If the gender of the brain and the genitals do not match, can transpeople return to an earlier self whom God knows?

4. The last verses of this psalm express anger against persecutors and a desire to be justified by God's strip search of the heart. Relate these emotions to transgender issues.

5. Ultimately, is suicide possible?

—*Maren C. Tirabassi*

32

TRANSGENDER RESOURCES FOR INDIVIDUAL AND COMMUNITY USE

PRACTICAL SUGGESTIONS FOR MAKING CONGREGATIONS MORE WELCOMING

MANY CONGREGATIONS THROUGHOUT THE ECUMENICAL CHURCH are led by faithful people of good intention, who have little knowledge about the issues of sexual justice and inclusivity. Often, church members believe that the concerns of nonheterosexuals and gender variant persons are just not an issue in their community. Research and experience informs us that this is not true. Transgender people are everywhere in our churches. Our language, assumptions, and practices have too often rendered them invisible. We choose not to see the diversity among us if we continue to act as if it is not there. Rare is the transgender person who can or should step forward seeking inclusion within a community that has never let anyone know that he/she will be safe, respected, and cherished as a child of God. If we want to become the whole people of God, then we must act as if we are. We must make specific, concrete acts of inclusion and liberation. Transgender people know that the world can be a hostile and dangerous place. Surely the church should be welcoming.

Below is a list of suggestions for local churches seeking to become welcoming of transgender persons. This list has been compiled by Pat Conover, a leader of trans-liberation in the United Church of Christ for many years, and author of the book *Transgender Good News,* New Wineskins Press, 2002.

Specific Things a Congregation Can Do to Welcome Transgender People

1. Create non–gender-designated bathrooms or make it clear that people should use the bathrooms of their presenting gender.

2. Create liturgies in which respondents are not divided by gender except in special circumstances.

3. Invite people to activities without designating them as men's or women's events.

4. Create the gender-specific activities and invitations that have a gender-related purpose, then reach out to known transgender people with specific welcome.

5. Use the transgender word in sermons or other worship settings in an affirming way. If you can't think of anything to build on, you might look again at some of the stories in this book or in Mary Boenke's book *Transforming Our Families: Real Stories about Transgender Loved Ones.*

6. Create a prayer group or a support group for people carrying a special burden and make sure it is a safe space for everyone.

7. Sponsor a lecture or discussion on transgender concerns in your church, or include an announcement about such events, or list the access information for the nearest transgender support group in your church newsletter.

8. Place an advertisement in your nearest gay and lesbian newspaper that lists your congregation as a church that welcomes gay, lesbian, bisexual, and transgender people. You may find some wonderful new members, but, at a minimum, this is a welcoming sign for those you already have, known or unknown.

9. Do some teacher training with your youth leaders so that they can understand how critical it can be to welcome those who are exploring their gender issues.

Perhaps the most important thing some congregations could do would be to create an appropriate adult Christian education program and encourage participation by anyone who wants to explore how their gender self-understandings are related to their faith. If people are doing their own gender work, it won't seem so strange to learn that transgender people are doing a special kind of gender work.

DEFINITIONS AND CONCEPTS

Gender identity is a concept that informs all of us about our lives all of the time. The social construction of meaning in words such as male and female, man and woman, feminine and masculine inform us about who we are and how we are to be in the world, long before we are born. Parents dream about what their child will look like, smell like, move like, sound like, and be like before he/she is even born. Rarely do these dreams exist without images of the child's future gender and the feelings and beliefs attached to that image.

Each of us lives within our own gender identity. How we live out our sense of being male or female, or some mixture of both, is part of the deepest core of our sexual/spiritual psyche. The transgender community is comprised of individuals who have courageously come forth to name that the label they were assigned at birth isn't right. It doesn't fit. In fact, it is damaging. Transgender people exist in every walk of life and express their gender identity in different manners, to varying degrees. Transpeople have much to teach.

Transsexuals are individuals who have a gender identity (the sense of being a man or a woman) different from their anatomical sex. They often seek medical treatment to change their physical attributes to correspond with their gender identity. This treatment may include hormone therapy, electrolysis, and surgery. Psychotherapy and real life experience in the new gender role is required for most medical treatment.

Cross-dressers wear clothing usually associated with the gender "opposite" to their anatomical sex. Cross-dressing may be part-time in the privacy of the person's own home, public, and even full-time. The difference is the cross-dressers' gender identity remains the same as their anatomical sex. They usually do not seek medical treatment. Erotic pleasure is sometimes the motivation for cross-dressing, especially in younger people. Cross-dressers can be attracted to either same-sex or opposite sex partners, or both.

Intersexed (hermaphroditic) individuals are born with genitals that show characteristics of both sexes or are opposite to their genetic sex. Many are surgically "corrected" in infancy, and some grow up to feel like they have had an essential part of themselves taken away without their consent. Even worse, many surgeries in infancy remove or diminish later sexual sensation and enjoyment.

Transgenderists live as members of the other sex, but without the extreme need or desire to alter their bodies that transsexuals experience. Some live permanently as members of the other sex, while others assume gender identities outside of the male-female two-gender model (third gender). Transgenderists often take hormones, some have other treatments (electrolysis), but few undergo surgical transformation.

Androgynes, Gender Benders, and Gender Blenders merge the characteristics of men and women in various ways that are sometimes subtle and sometimes shocking.

Drag kings and drag queens present larger-than-life images of men and women, exaggerating gender stereotypes for entertainment, attention, or self-gratification.

Transpeople/transgendered people are group nouns that are often used to describe all transgendered and transsexual people (all the above).

RECOMMENDED READINGS, ORGANIZATIONS AND WEB SITES

Books

Boenke, Mary. *Transforming Our Families: Real Stories About Transgendered Loved Ones.* Imperial Beach, Calif.: Walter Trook Publishing, 1999.

Brown, Mildred, and Chloe Rounsley. *True Selves: Understanding Transsexualism—For Families, Friends, Coworkers, and Helping Professionals.* SanFrancisco: Jossey-Bass, 1996.

Cameron, Loren. *Body Alchemy: Transsexual Portraits.* Pittsburgh: Cleis Press, 1996.

Conover, Pat. *Transgender Good News.* Silver Spring, Md.: New Wineskins Press, 2002.

Mollenkott, Virginia Ramey. *Omni-gender: A Trans-religious Approach.* Cleveland: Pilgrim Press, 2001.

Sheridan, Vanessa. *Crossing Over: Liberating the Transgender Christian.* Cleveland: Pilgrim Press. 2001.

Printed Resources

The Harry Benjamin International Gender Dysphoria Association, Inc. *Standards of Care for Gender Identity Disorders,* sixth version, February 2001.

PFLAG Transgender Resource Packet, a collection of articles, information, and contacts. PFLAG, www.pflag.org, 202-467-8180.

Transgender Pocket, a packet of information particularly useful for UCC members and congregations, The UCC Coalition for LGBT Concerns, ONACoord@UCCcoalition.org, 508-856-9316.

"Transgender Tapestry," a magazine of the International Foundation for Gender Education, www.ifge.org.

Organizations and Web Sites

At one: A Network of Transgender People in the United Church of Christ, Monica Smith (smithm@ucc.org), 216-736-3218.

FTM (Female-to-Male) International (www.ftm-into.org), 415-553-5987.

GenderPac (www.gpac.org), 202-462-6610.

The International Foundation for Gender Education (www.ifge.org), IFGE, PO Box 540229, Waltham, MA 02454-0229, 781-899-2212.

Parents and Friends of Lesbians and Gays (PFLAG), www.pflag.org, 202-467-8180.

The United Church of Christ Coalition for LGBT Concerns, www.UCCcoalition.org, 800-653-0799.

Transcendence Gospel Choir, Directors: Ashley Moore and Yvonne Evans, www.tgchoir.org, tgc@tgchoir.org, 510-682-7763.

www.annelawrence.com/twr/

www.emergenceministries.org

http://transsexual.org/links.html

LIST OF CONTRIBUTORS

Ms. Rose A. (pseudonym)

Ms. Dzintra Alksnitis

Rev. Judith Ann Becker

Dr. Anne L. Boedecker

Ms. Jennifer Linda Brooks

Ms. Janice Josephine Carney

Ms. Anna Mae Carolyne

Rev. Ann B. Day

Mr. Terry Dresser

Mr. Chris R. Glaser

Ms. Judith Hanlon

Ms. Lisa Hartley

Ms. Lauren Haywood

Ms. Audra Lynn Imboden

Rev. Joanna Louise

Ms. Christine Loveless

Ms. Ella Matheson (pseudonym)

Mr. Nickolas Jakob McDaniel

Ms. Ashley Moore

Mr. Jacob Nash

Rev. Karen Oliveto

Mr. Lewis Christopher Payne

Ms. Pamela Ann Reed

Rev. Stephanie Rodriguez

Ms. Barbara Satin

Rev. Donna Schaper

Rev. David H. Schmidt

Rev. Bran Scott

Rev. Sheryl Stewart

Rev. John H. Thomas

Rev. Dr. Leanne M. Tigert

Rev. Maren C. Tirabassi

Rev. David A. Travers

Ms. Leslie Walter

Related Titles from The Pilgrim Press

CROSSING OVER
Liberating the Transgendered Christian
VANESSA SHERIDAN

Transgendered author Sheridan reflects on her experience and the experiences of others in order to describe the realities and dispel the myths about those who are transgendered. She encourages transgendered people to seek sources of spiritual strength and join the struggle for justice in the church and the larger society. 2003 Lambda Literary Award finalist.

ISBN 0-8298-1446-9/Paper/160 pages/$16.00

OMNIGENDER
A Trans-Religious Approach
VIRGINIA RAMEY MOLLENKOTT

Mollenkott examines the problems inherent in our society's bipolar concept of gender identity. *Omnigender* bridges traditional religious doctrine and secular postmodern theory, and offers fresh ways of thinking about gender in our society. Winner of a 2002 Lambda Literary Award.

ISBN 0-8298-1422-1/Cloth with jacket/208 pages/$18.00

TRANS-GENDERED
Theology, Ministry, and Communities of Faith
JUSTIN TANIS

Tanis, a transgendered clergyperson, seeks to explore the spiritual nature of transgendered persons, to listen to the stories of others like himself, and to give a positive voice to the community. 2003 Lambda Literary Award finalist.

ISBN 0-8298-1528-7/Paper/208 pages/$19.00

To order these or any other books from The Pilgrim Press, call or write to:

The Pilgrim Press
700 Prospect Avenue
Cleveland, Ohio 44115-1100

PHONE ORDERS: 800-537-3394 (M–F, 8:30 AM–4:30 PM ET)

FAX ORDERS: 216-736-2206

Please include shipping charges of $5.00 for the first book and 75¢ for each additional book.

OR ORDER FROM OUR WEB SITE AT WWW.THEPILGRIMPRESS.COM.

Prices subject to change without notice.